All in Our Places

Feminist Challenges in Elementary School Classrooms

Carla Washburne Rensenbrink

ROWMAN & LITTLEFIELD PUBLISHERS, INC.
Lanham • Boulder • New York • Oxford

#44750666

ROWMAN & LITTLEFIELD PUBLISHERS, INC.

Published in the United States of America
by Rowman & Littlefield Publishers, Inc.
4720 Boston Way, Lanham, Maryland 20706
http://www.rowmanlittlefield.com

12 Hid's Copse Road, Cumnor Hill
Oxford OX2 9JJ, England

British Cataloguing in Publication Information Available

Library of Congress Cataloging-in-Publication Data
Rensenbrink, Carla Washburne, 1937–
    All in our places : feminist challenges in elementary school classrooms / Carla Washburne Rensenbrink.
        p. cm.
    Includes bibliographical references and index.
    ISBN 0-8476-9478-X (alk. paper)—ISBN 0-8476-9479-8 (pbk. : alk. paper)
        1. Sexism in education—United States. 2. Women teachers—United States—Social conditions. 3. Discrimination in education—United States. 4. Education (Elementary)—Social aspects—United States. I. Title: Feminist challenges in elementary school classrooms. II. Title.

    LC212.82 .R45 2001
    306.43'2'0973—dc21

                                                                00-059223

Printed in the United States of America

∞™ The paper used in this publication meets the minimum requirements of American National Standard for Information Sciences—Permanence of Paper for Printed Library Materials, ANSI/NISO Z.39.48–1992.

All in Our Places

for Lucy, Marcia, Rosemary

Contents

Preface

Next door to the elementary school where I taught for many years there was a small mom-and-pop store. Mom and Pop were crusty, hardworking people. They put in long hours. When we teachers went in to buy a sandwich or a cup of coffee that was marginally fresher than ours, they would make wry comments about how short our day was, how numerous our vacations, how soft our job. *Then,* their daughter became a first grade teacher in a nearby town. Gradually, their tune changed. They became sympathetic and respectful. They would ask how things were going next door. When we came in to grab a bite between school and a meeting, they would say, "Here you go, Teach. You need it."

You have to be very close, I think, to a person who is an elementary school teacher in order to have an inkling of the demands of the job. Elementary school teaching, like other forms of "women's work," is devalued and made invisible in this culture. The complexity and difficulty of the job are vastly misunderstood and underestimated.

In this book, I try to get closer to that work through a careful examination of three classrooms. I present life histories of the three teachers and try to foreground their insights, questions, and goals as we look together at their teaching practice. The teachers all call themselves *feminists,* and they are concerned about the meaning of that term in their teaching. They try to understand all their students and to build relationships with them. They strive to move beyond tolerance to a true celebration of differences and to the creation of community. They question their own practice and struggle to find ways to teach, to empower, and to love their students.

Their classrooms are full of energy, noise, humor, pain, love, purpose, and confusion. There is always a lot more going on than any teacher can possibly know, and even with the extra eyes of the researcher, only a small part of this intricate, microcosmic world can be recorded and examined. It is important to keep in mind that this overwhelming number of events and amount of detail is the reality of teaching—and of research about teaching.

This account is also the story of my own changing perspective, which came about as a by-product of doing research. I started with a long-standing interest in gender issues, but I began to see more clearly how gender is complicated by and inseparable from other factors—race, class, sexuality, ability, wealth. I tried to keep multiple perspectives in mind, but perhaps the hardest thing for me was to recognize how sometimes I did *not* see what was perfectly plain to someone else or failed to make room for another perspective. Talking with the teachers and getting feedback from friends and colleagues have helped me fill in some gaps, see a little more deeply, be more conscious of how my own perspective can blind me to certain things. In this book I will show some of the things I missed or misunderstood and how I came back to them later and saw them differently—in hopes of presenting an ever-broadening perspective. I am afraid that many gaps and blind spots remain. As teachers, there is so much that we need to know, so much we do not—or cannot—see. These three teachers, because of their openness, reflectiveness, and self-awareness, can, I believe, help us to see more.

The teachers in this study work in very different settings in and around a large eastern city: Lucy in a suburb, Rosemary in a large town, and Marcia in the inner city. To give a preliminary sense of the variation in the teachers' style of teaching, their curricular interests, and their modes of discipline, here—in the order in which I encountered them—are glimpses into each classroom.

Lucy is stooping over Raina's desk, intent on the child's writing. Raina has written an illustrated book about herself and her friend Debbie, entitled *Raina and Debbie Get Kidnapped*. She is about to publish it in the classroom. Lucy's appreciation and enjoyment of Raina's work are evident. The other children in this second grade class are involved in a wide variety of activities: writing, reading, playing chess, working with clay. There is a hum of activity. Occasionally Lucy glances at the block corner, which has the potential to disrupt the peace, checking on Reggie, Neil, and Vic.

Rosemary has pulled her class together in a rough circle. She and her fifth graders are discussing an article on domestic violence among military personnel that Ricky has been reporting on for current events. Rosemary urges the children to look at the story critically, to see different perspectives, to relate this story to their own lives. She makes occasional wry, joking comments—directed most often at Henry and Heather—to keep the children focused and involved.

Marcia sits in a child-size chair at one of the children's tables, going over homework folders. Her first and second graders are grouped together nearby. They have organized themselves for their daily show-and-tell. It is Rosita's turn to be in charge. She calls on a girl, then a boy, then a girl, in a pattern of strict alternation. One by one the children stand next to Rosita and tell the group about what they did after school yesterday, which of their friends they saw, what they heard on the news—or they pull out some object hidden under a sweatshirt or in a backpack to show the class. Marcia frequently looks up from her papers and directs a comment or a question to the speaker. Sitting on the floor at her knee is Roland, whom Marcia removed from the group because he was pinching.

Throughout this study these three teachers have shown great generosity and courage by letting me into their classrooms. That meant, for them, a loss of privacy, the cancellation of those few minutes they might have had to themselves when the children were at art or recess, and the need to keep an extra, hovering presence in mind. For many teachers it is important to be able to close the classroom door and concentrate on their students. I interrupted that intimacy while I was there, participating and observing. Sometimes I saw what was not meant to be seen—a flair of anger, a peculiar habit, some private likes and dislikes. And I was necessarily raising questions—asking the teacher why she did this or that, how she interpreted a particular event, how she planned to deal with a certain situation. When I wasn't questioning—on days I wasn't there—this project still inevitably gave rise to a lot of self-reflection and questioning. But all three teachers, even at the end of a demanding school day, were willing to sit down and talk. They could still find the energy to discuss their kids, their lives, their work.

I hope readers will share my admiration for these teachers. They are doing a job that requires courage, creativity, intelligence, energy, and persistence—and these qualities are not just called on at rare moments, but daily and hourly. This project reminded me of how the work of teaching is both extraordinary and ordinary. I hope that teachers reading this book will find new insights for their teaching practice and that they also will recognize themselves in these three teachers. I hope that these stories will remind teachers of the ordinary extraordinariness of the work they do.

I am deeply grateful to the three real teachers who stand behind Lucy, Rosemary, and Marcia. There are many other people whose help and encouragement have been crucial in writing this book. I'm starting at the beginning when I mention my husband, John Rensenbrink. Many ideas in this book stem directly or indirectly from conversations with him. My daughters, Kathryn, Greta, and Liz, have given their support, their insights, and their sometimes wry commentary.

From our first meeting and throughout this project, Kathleen Weiler has challenged my thinking, encouraged me in many ways, and not let me give up. Frances Maher shared invaluable experiences from her own research with feminist teachers and helped me find new ways of understanding and interpreting the three teachers I like to think of as mine. The thoughtful critique of Margo Okazawa-Rey made me take a hard look at my own positioning in this book and rethink the way I wrote much of it.

There are other people to whom I am also very grateful for precious support in the form of exchanging ideas or reading and reacting to what I had written. Among them are Eileen Landay, Carol Sperry, Joseph Maxwell, Elaine Schear, Ann Rath, Beverly Smith, Catherine Krupnick, Courtney Cazden, Barbara Houston, and Nona Lyons. And finally, Karen Maloney's energy and perspicacity have made it possible to complete this book.

1

Feminism and Teaching

I feel as if I'm constantly aware of gender issues—more than any other issue [in the classroom].

—Lucy

I hate sex role stereotyping—I hate that boys don't want to do things with girls. They don't want to sit next to them. They don't want to play with them.

—Rosemary

Girls can do anything boys can do—and they can do better!

—Marcia

Gender seemed a logical focus for my research on the lives and work of three feminist teachers. Gender is such a powerful, though often unremarked, presence in a school day. The day may begin with the greeting, "Good morning, boys and girls," and proceed through boys' and girls' lines, segregated playground activities, and a curriculum in which women are largely absent. The majority of teachers are women, as they have been for more than 100 years in this country, yet men still hold most of the decision-making roles as principals and superintendents, professors and deans in schools of education.

In the classrooms I observed for this project, I saw children actively working out their ideas of gender and of self-identity. But these ideas were always complicated by race, class, sexuality, and other subject positions. The tensions, divisions, and expectations that these young children were sometimes surprisingly aware of are more often associated with adolescence, which has lately been the focus of our alarmed attention in this country. But there is a continuity between the awareness and concerns of students in elementary school and issues more often associated with middle school students: identity, stereotyping, racism, homophobia, anorexia, violence, and suicide. And, as one of the teachers in this study said, "We can't *start* unteaching prejudice in the middle school."

Gender, then, seemed to be only the opening wedge into a look at the broad and deep issues that are being worked out in our schools, as they are in our society generally. The lives and work of Marcia, Lucy, and Rosemary[1] will offer insights, encouragement, and perhaps some answers. The issues raised in their classrooms are challenging and complicated. They do not offer easy solutions, although they point to the questions that need further asking, and they indicate exciting possibilities.

Too often the education that we want to be engrossing, enlarging, and liberating turns out to be stultifying, overly competitive, and seemingly careless of individual students. We are horrified by the gross inequities of our school systems and by the terrifying outbreaks of violence in schools, even in highly regarded schools like Columbine High School. These are symptoms of a system in serious trouble. How can we put our trust in reform efforts based on a narrowing discourse of learning standards, testing outcomes, and further testing of teachers? Will this reform effort begin to *touch* the deeper problems? Might it not—with its insistence on competitiveness at the core of our educational system—actually exacerbate the problems we already face?

We live in a society where profit is the organizing principle by which large-scale decisions are made, values assigned, and persons judged. According to this principle children seem beneath notice. The richest society the world has ever known leaves one-quarter of its children in poverty. By the nature of their work, teachers, who devote their lives to educating children, struggle against this principle. At the same time, they are at the center of a contradiction. They can, by the decisions they make, socialize or liberate their students. They can lead students to accept or to take a critical view of the values of our society. They can aim for the replication or the transformation of that society. In these three classrooms the teachers try, within the constraints of the public school system, to organize the communal life around the needs of the children and their hopes for their students' futures.

In analyzing the classrooms presented in this book and in drawing lessons and inspiration from them, I have found feminist theory useful because it starts from the fact of gender but broadens to incorporate issues of race, sexuality, class, and other subject positions. At different times in my research I relied on a variety of approaches to feminist theory that seemed most helpful in particular contexts. In the section that follows, I present several of these approaches, organizing them around a series of questions that seem to be the driving force behind each approach and then relating these questions to issues in education. These questions will be raised again in the case studies that follow in an attempt to contribute to the ongoing conversation about feminism and teaching.

I end the chapter by describing how I set up this project, how I chose the three teachers, and what it was like for me as a teacher to be a researcher as well.

QUESTIONS FEMINISM RAISES ABOUT EDUCATION

In her book *Feminist Thought* (1989) Rosemary Tong reviews many different approaches to feminist thinking. She uses the image of a kaleidoscope to capture her sense of an overlapping and constantly changing pattern. "What makes feminist thought liberating," she says, "is its vitality, its refusal to stop changing, to stop growing" (237).

Feminist thought on the subject of education has also been both changing and overlapping. It is interesting, and somewhat discouraging, that, although the questions and concerns of feminists have deepened and broadened and become more complex since the late 1960s, none of the questions that were posed then can really be counted as answered, none of the problems finally solved. In other words, the concerns of the early movement are still with us, although the energy of some feminists has moved on to other issues. For instance, questions of equal opportunities for female students remain a vital and sometimes burning issue for many teachers and students, while other thinkers are questioning standard definitions of gender itself. This sort of range and complexity suggests the need for a broad, inclusive, multifaceted approach to issues of feminism and teaching.

The review that follows, of questions that feminism has to ask about education, deals with some major areas. I have illustrated each group of questions with examples from the case studies, to show the many ways feminist questions are relevant in the classroom. These same questions were also part of my own teaching, my struggles with fairness and expectations, my efforts to create a better world in my classroom, and my desire to empower my students to take on their own battles. I realized as I worked through this chapter that to some extent, this sequence of questions also reflects my own changing and developing ideas about feminism. But here too, the later questions do not obliterate or ultimately answer the earlier ones. Rather they look at the core issues of feminism with a different turn of the kaleidoscope.

Questions about Equity and Sex-Role Stereotyping in Education

When I began teaching in 1970, I had just begun to connect with the Women's Liberation Movement and to recognize my own feminism. In fact, it was the Women's Movement that "freed" me, as a young mother, to think about working outside of the home and ultimately led me to teaching. In my mind, the struggle toward my own liberation was entwined with the way I imagined I could liberate children from the narrow, dry, decontextualized schooling I had experienced.

Beginning in the late 1960s, women (not for the first time) began to question women's second-class status and current notions of what women ought to be. They questioned the "naturalness" of women's role in society. They saw "woman's place" as resulting from differential expectations that led to different educational paths and to exclusion from the realms of politics, business, and the professions. They attempted to change male/female power relationships through political and legal reform. Gradually, these ideas were taken up by teachers and parents. What did such ideas suggest about what was going on in schools?

Some of the issues first seized on were questions of sex-role stereotyping, equity, and access. For instance, observers found far more limited opportunities for girls in sports—less money, less time, less choice, and less media coverage. Also, girls were often not expected to do well in math and science, courses that were seen as essentially masculine. Girls' performance in these areas seemed to match expectations, but their lower achievement had raised little concern. On the other hand—in that reversal that often reveals sexist practice—there was much concern over boys' lesser achievement in reading and writing. As Rosemary, one of the teachers in this study, recalled, "No one felt it was OK for boys not to learn to read and write." In the classroom, observers found that teachers paid more attention to boys and that boys took up more of the "airtime." Some courses were explicitly sex-typed: Girls were denied access to "male" courses like industrial arts, whereas boys were admitted, but did not flock, to "female" courses like home economics.

Feminists and others looked at images in textbooks and were shocked at the presentation of girls as weak and fearful and of women as only secretaries, nurses, teachers, or mothers in aprons. In the 1970s Lucy picked up her daughter's second grade reader and happened to notice that all the main characters were boys. Her reaction—"I was *furious!*"—marked the beginning of her feminist consciousness.

Parents and educators began to wonder about the connections between such limited role models in school texts and women's lesser status in society. In schools almost all the administrators were men and almost all the elementary school teachers were women. There was bias in "standardized" tests and in career counseling. One instrument, designed to pinpoint career preferences, came in two formats—one pink and one blue.

Although work on identifying and rectifying equity issues has been going on for some time now, it can still be seen as work only begun, as *The AAUW Report: How Schools Shortchange Girls* (1992) and Myra and David Sadker's book *Failing at Fairness: How Our Schools Cheat Girls* (1994) show. Take, for example, the question of the teacher distributing her energy and attention equally among boys and girls. In the three classrooms I observed the teachers were highly conscious of this issue. But it is not so easy to correct. "Simple" equality runs so much against the grain of our cultural expectations (children's as well as teachers') and of our established patterns of behavior that boys in these classes *still* got more than their share of teacher time. The most equal example I witnessed, in fact, was in Marcia's first grade class when the children were in charge of show-and-tell. They themselves had decided to take turns calling on a boy, then a girl. When Rodrigo was the leader, he would say to a pal, "I can't call on you now 'cause you're a boy."

In the struggle to provide equality for girls there has been an underlying assumption (sometimes questioned, sometimes not) that what girls want is what boys have, what women want is what men have. In this model it is the girls who have to change, but it is also the girls who stand to gain, as they are encouraged to be more confident and to take on new roles, whereas boys stand to lose former privileges. This model seemed to be what was in Sarah's mind, one of the first teachers I interviewed. She did not want to participate as a case study teacher, because, she said, although she thought of herself as a feminist, she did not think of herself as a feminist *teacher*. She thought being a feminist teacher would imply greater concern for the girls and less for the boys in her class. Sarah hits on an assumption many people make about feminism—that it is concerned with broadening opportunities only for girls and women.

The teachers in this study will disprove this assumption. All three were concerned about how limiting current gender stereotypes are for both boys and girls. Rosemary helps the quieter kids in her class (mostly but not all girls) to speak up and to act as leaders; she also encourages all her fifth graders to help out in the kindergarten, and boys who might not have volunteered without her urging find this project rewarding. In this way Rosemary helps children to explore different possibilities for themselves and to develop a broader, more accepting sense of who they are and who others might be.

Questions Rising from a Focus on Girls and Women in Education

One criticism of the early equity movement was that it seemed to see girls only in relation to boys, or even as less than boys. The struggle for equality seemed to push girls to be more like boys in order for them to succeed in school and in future careers. Is this what schools should focus on—what girls need to know in order to succeed in the terms laid out by a male-dominated society? Or is there a different way to look at this question? What sort of picture would be created by a focus on girls and women themselves and a consideration of how they should be taught? Their experience, history, arts, "ways of knowing," and particular strengths have been left out of the curriculum.

Adrienne Rich asked, "What does a woman need to know?"

> Does she not, as a self-conscious, self-defining human being, need a knowledge of her own history, her much-politicized biology, an awareness of the creative work of women of the past, the skills and crafts and techniques and powers exercised by women in different times and cultures, a knowledge of women's rebellions and organized movements against our oppression and how they have been routed or diminished? Without such knowledge women live and have lived without context, vulnerable to the projections of male fantasy, male prescriptions for us, estranged from our own experience because our education has not reflected or echoed it. (Rich 1979, 240)

The effort to recover such knowledge has been made more difficult by the degree to which women's history has been buried in a society in which men hold the greater share of power. Men define women and assign to them certain roles based on their biological differences from men. These roles have traditionally included housework, emotional work, nurturing, care of the old and the young, and teaching—at least, teaching young children. Eventually such roles come to be seen as "natural"— things women are naturally better at. We are surrounded by images of women that fit this expectation, so we don't often stop to ask ourselves, Were women *born* that way? Or have they just adapted to the limited opportunities assigned or offered to them? I asked Lucy if she thought it was "natural" for women to do certain things better than men. She replied, "I don't know . . . I guess those are the things men don't want to do."

The submersion of women in male-dominated society is evident in our language in the use of the presumably generic he/man (*Man and His Symbols, The Descent of Man*)—which we have been instructed to interpret as including women. This was not lost on Nora, a second grader in Lucy's class who was trilingual and unusually aware of language. One day she came over to where I was sitting with Rosie and pointed to the word *human* on Rosie's spelling paper.

> Nora said, "You know what bothers me? This word has *man* in it—*woman* has *man* in it."
> "Yes," I said, "and what about *person*?"
> "Yeah, *son*. What about words for us?" she asked.

We came up with *girl* and *lady* as the only "words for us" that we could think of.

Carol Gilligan's book *In a Different Voice* (1982) is often viewed as path-breaking. She observed that the preponderance of psychological and developmental studies had been done with male subjects. The tests had been "normed" on the male sample so that in many cases females taking the same tests did not do as well or showed results that were dismissed as erratic. Gilligan focused on female subjects and found different explanations for the erratic results. She provided evidence that many women make moral choices on different bases than men—that women typically are more concerned with caring relationships than with more abstract applications of law and justice. In reaching a decision women tend to consider individual factors and the overall context.

Stages in women's intellectual development, based on women's experience of the world and their position in it, are detailed in *Women's Ways of Knowing* (1986), by Mary Belenky, Blythe Clinchy, Nancy Goldberger, and Jill Tarule. The authors found that women of all ages, classes, ethnicities, and levels of education—any woman—"needs to know that she is capable of intelligent thought, and she needs to know it right away" (193). Their work shows again the importance for women of connection and context in learning and teaching. These concepts are important ones for all the teachers in this study.

Feminist educators have wanted to recover women's history, art forms, and literature and to use materials from these new sources in schools. Rosemary has worked on curricular materials that place greater emphasis on women's experience as part of history and on women writers and thinkers in all areas of the curriculum. Using these recovered resources constitutes a serious change in curriculum, a different idea of what knowledge is important, what *all* our children need to know.

Feminist efforts have raised concerns that had previously been submerged and not seen as major problems because they happened mostly to women and children. Public awareness of the scope of domestic violence against children and women has increased because of greater consciousness and media attention. Concerns about children have led to the ongoing battle for safe, quality day care. In the three classrooms that I studied, the question of safety loomed large, and the teachers found themselves dealing daily with issues of violence in the children's lives at home, on the streets, and even in school. Under the often-threatening circumstances of contemporary life, they were concerned about preserving the health and safety of their children and their freedom to grow and thrive.

Jane Roland Martin, partly in response to such threatening circumstances in and out of schools, has imagined and described a very different kind of school in her book *Schoolhome: Rethinking Schools for Changing Families* (1992). Her school is created around the "three Cs" of care, concern, and connection. In this school the curriculum includes many forms of knowledge traditionally associated with women and integrates them with more conventional school subjects.

In *The Challenge to Care in Schools: An Alternative Approach to Education* (1992), Nel Noddings criticizes contemporary schools for their narrow focus on verbal and mathematical skills and their overemphasis on academic success. She proposes changes to the structure of the school day and an additional curriculum based on "centers of care" expanding outward from the self. Since the traditional disciplines and the structures and curricula of most schools have been designed by and for men, she conceptualizes her changes as what schools might look like "if, for example, women rather than men had designed them" (61).

A question for contemporary feminists is how the efforts to value women as something other than lesser men and to look at their unique strengths, abilities, and values puts them into a box again. This question has a long history in the field of education. In the nineteenth century, at a time when women were increasingly becoming schoolteachers, a great deal of advice literature was written for women—in particular middle-class White women—holding them up to the standard of True Womanhood. This ideal of Womanhood exalted four emblematic qualities: piety, purity, submissiveness, and domesticity. Proponents of women as teachers, such as Catharine Beecher, Henry Barnard, Horace Mann, and others, found that these qualities were precisely the ones that would make women good teachers, particularly of young children. Indeed, they found that women were "naturally" suited for the job (Sklar 1973).

Catharine Beecher promoted the idea of women as teachers by arguing that teaching was a good preparation for motherhood. This problematic association has persisted. All three teachers in this study, whether or not they were mothers, made connections between mothering and teaching that will come up in the case studies.

A vital question for feminists—and one with important implications for all teachers—is the degree to which we see these "female" qualities as natural or as cultural, as biologically determined or as imposed by the requirements of the culture. In her book entitled *Am I That Name?: Feminism and the Category of 'Women' in History* (1988), Denise Riley looks at the different ways women have been viewed from the fourteenth century to the present day. She finds that the category "women" has changed so much during different times and places that it seems not to contain any permanent characteristics other than physical ones.

Questions about Education Rising from Diverse Perspectives

Some of the efforts by women to redefine women failed to take into account the broad range of people who are women. Both the current wave of the Women's Movement and the earlier movement in the nineteenth century have been criticized for being racist in that they were largely organized around the perceptions, experiences, and needs of White, middle-class women and tended to be relatively insouciant about other women.

Black feminism also has a long history, going back at least to Maria W. Stewart, Sojourner Truth, and Anna Julia Cooper in the nineteenth century (Collins 1991). Many Black feminists have addressed issues in education. Anna Julia Cooper had a varied career as a teacher, administrator, and inspirer of African American students. Her assessment of the situation of girls in school and her hopes for leadership among Black women led to her demand that schools provide "Not the boys less, but the girls more" (Titone and Maloney, 88).

A particular reason for wanting to include Marcia as an African American[2] woman in this project was the fact that teaching has historically occupied a somewhat different position in the Black community than it has in the White community. From the period of slavery in this country, when it was illegal and horribly punishable for enslaved people to learn to read, there has been a heritage of resistance connected with teaching. bell hooks (1989) describes her favorite high school teacher, Miss Annie Mae Moore, who taught in the segregated schools of the South. Miss Moore helped her students look critically at the White supremacist world surrounding them and offered them an "oppositional worldview."

Another strong emphasis among African American educators has been the goal of "raising the race" (Collins 1991, hooks 1989). Education is seen as a way out of oppression, as a door opening on a broader world, and as a way of creating leaders who will in their turn work to benefit their people. Already in first grade, Marcia's students, most of whom are children of color, are learning their place in the community and their obligations to it.

Most White teachers would not think of themselves as raising the race, and some might criticize such a goal. Nor would they be apt to see how White are the curricula and structures of our public schools or how teaching within these parameters unconsciously, but undeniably, favors children who are White.

Kathleen Weiler observed that none of the teachers whom she interviewed for her book *Women Teaching for Change* (1988) said anything like, "Of course I'm white and that has deeply affected me" (76). Nor was this pointed out by any of the teachers I interviewed. White people tend not to think of race unless we are thinking of *other* races—then it becomes an issue. That is because White is the norm in this society, and we see difference in relation to the norm. The norm is privileged—White people are privileged—because in so many ways we conform to the norm without even thinking about it. It is very uncomfortable to acknowledge this privilege, which Peggy McIntosh (1989) claims we wear as an "invisible knapsack." We would rather, she says, acknowledge that others are dis-advantaged than that we ourselves are privileged.

Lisa Delpit shows how dangerous this blindness is when we are teaching *Other People's Children* (1995) and how important it is for teachers to recognize and be knowledgeable about cultural differences. In my first case study Lucy struggled to understand and to teach an African American child. I identified with her struggles but could not help with her understanding. Both of us, as I could see later, were hampered by our inadequate information on issues of race and culture—and by our own unconscious assumptions.

The need to uncover, face, and change some of those assumptions became a challenge for me as a researcher trying to understand and represent the life and work of a White teacher in a multicultural classroom and that of an African American teacher. A similar challenge was posed by my work with Rosemary, a lesbian teacher who is "out" to her school. She courageously takes on the varying reactions of colleagues, parents, and students to that aspect of herself. As will be clear from her story, Rosemary sometimes sees the world from a different angle because she is a lesbian. She wants others to be able to see that too.

In an effort to explore diverse points of view, I wanted to include a teacher who is a lesbian and a teacher who is a woman of color, as well as a teacher who is White and heterosexual. The class background of the three teachers also varies, as their life histories will show. These identities do not in my mind, or in the minds of the teachers themselves, represent hardened or unchanging viewpoints. These differences don't *always* make a difference. But sometimes they do, and these teachers brought from their own experience of the world knowledge, references, and interpretations that were new to me. They had what Sandra Harding calls an "epistemological advantage." Their experience enabled them to understand things that I could not—without their help. In terms of knowledge, Harding sees an advantage to "starting from the lives of those who have been devalued, neglected, excluded from the center of the social order" (1991, 211). Women are part of this group, and feminists have long criticized hierarchical knowledge, academic disciplines, rules of conduct, and other aspects of knowledge that were supposed to be neutral or universal but were in fact male-centered. Other groups can claim the same "epistemological advantage."

A serious attempt to understand the perspective of one who is "other" can have an equal and opposite effect: the need to examine one's own positionality. Some recent educational literature examines Whiteness itself and how feminism—like other ways of thought in this culture—tends to keep Whiteness at its core and to see "others" insofar as they differ from that norm, rather than placing the "others" at the center and critiquing the norm of Whiteness from their point of view.

Frances A. Maher and Mary Kay Tetreault interviewed eighteen feminist college professors in a variety of institutions for their book *The Feminist Classroom* (1994). Their early encounters with these professors forced the authors to reexamine their own expectations about feminist teaching and led them to recognize that their ideal of a "democratic and cooperative feminist teacher had been an example of our mistaking the experience of white middle-class women like ourselves for gendered universals" (15). They found they needed to revise their methodology. Still later they revisited their data and wrote an article (Maher and Tetreault 1997) foregrounding issues of Whiteness that they felt they had not sufficiently seen before in the same classrooms.

Although I had been forewarned by these authors, I sometimes fell into a similar trap. On several occasions, in talking with the case study teachers, I was brought up against their different interpretations of an event or a motivation or a statement—which jolted me into examining the assumptions behind my own interpretations. In a similar way the diversity of women's voices has interrogated the assumptions of the earlier Women's Movement and greatly broadened its concerns.

Questions about Teaching and Social Change

Feminism, growing out of the Women's Liberation Movement, has always meant social change and has offered different ways of working toward such change. In the 1970s feminist teachers began their efforts toward change by trying to create greater fairness in the curriculum, in course offerings, and in their treatment of boys and girls—as if with these inequities removed, schools would then be able to provide equal opportunities for girls and boys. In their hopes for change, feminist teachers paid inadequate attention to the enormous weight of inequities students already bring to school or to the complex and difficult challenge of creating equal opportunities in a very unequal world.

Kathleen Weiler's study of *Women Teaching for Change* (1988) looked at the lives and work of a group of high school teachers. She examined the ways these women's lives were constrained by the sexism, racism, and classism of this society and also the ways these teachers countered those limitations in themselves and in their work. They encouraged their students to raise critical questions and to develop a greater sense of their own possibilities.

Similar constraints and struggles will be seen in the three teachers of this study, as they resist the factors that keep us "all in our places." Their stories of their families, the decisions they made about their own lives, and their work itself reveal these constraints. But these are women who also see in their role as elementary school teachers wider possibilities for themselves and for the children they relate to daily in their classrooms.

Unfortunately, teachers—particularly elementary school teachers—are not ordinarily seen as activists, as looking beyond their classrooms, as having the kind of knowledge required to conceptualize change. Dan C. Lortie, for example in his 1975 book, *Schoolteacher: A Sociological Study*, described teachers as typically conservative, individualistic, and presentist in their orientation (212). Kathleen Casey portrays a very different sort of teacher in her book *I Answer with My Life: Life Histories of Women Teachers Working for Social Change* (1993). Casey focused on the place of political action in the lives and work of progressive teachers whose commitment to teaching extended beyond their classrooms. Feminism is a significant subtext in the stories of these activist teachers.

The teachers in my study also refute Lortie's findings. Rosemary, for instance, involved her fifth graders in discussing the issues of the day and tried to empower them to speak up for themselves and work for social change—even if it was only protesting to the principal that the sub had treated the girls in the class unfairly.

Questions about Gender Roles and the Power of Discourse in Education

Schools have traditionally used gender as a means of social control. Gender is kept in the forefront by the litany of "boys and girls" or more rarely "girls and boys," by girls' and boys' lines, girls' and boys' classes, gender divisions on the playground, and the way preferences bifurcate, so that what girls like, boys will scorn, and vice versa. This emphasis reconstitutes gender as we know it daily and hourly in school and underscores the power of expectations and of language in shaping our ideas of ourselves.

Language, expectations, curriculum, and the structure of school systems all combine to form a discourse that both extends and limits those who participate in it. We gradually learn this discourse as we go to school. We learn how we are expected to behave depending on our gender, class, race, and ability as a student. Most of this information is passed on to us by invisible means, and we are not very aware of it. We can go along with it or resist it, but to think *outside* of a given and familiar discourse is very difficult.

In this society the familiar discourse presents us with masculinity and femininity as polar opposites like black and white, Black and White, right and wrong, and success and failure. The pairs of any of these dichotomies are interlocked so that it is hard to conceive of one without the other as a contrast. The interlocked pairs also help keep each other in place. Given this kind of thinking, if women are to be nurturing, then men must be tough. Postmodern thinking tries to push beyond this binary, either/or habit of mind toward a greater recognition of complexity, contradiction, and multiplicity.

Sandra Harding points out that we must find ways to move beyond a male/female opposition. Earlier versions of feminism tended to emphasize the domination of men in a patriarchal society, whereas later versions are developing "new analyses of gender relations as they have historically been constructed through imperialism, class exploitation, and the control of sexuality. These studies . . . historicize, contextualize within history, the male supremacy that has been the particularly prevalent and insufferable part of gender relations" (1991, x). Such thinking would tend to move feminism beyond blaming men to taking a broader look at the construction of gender in this society.

Earlier forms of feminism emphasized growth and liberation for females while tending to ignore necessary, corollary changes in our expectations for boys and men. The burden for change thus remained only on girls and women. More recent literature has also looked at how boys suffer from what William Pollack calls a "gender straitjacket" (Matchan 2000). A postmodern approach stresses the interlocking character of our conventional definitions of male and female, Black and White, gay and straight—and the need to reexamine both.

Gender differences were often mentioned by the teachers in this study as creating a major challenge. "How can you treat boys and girls the same, when they are so different?" asked Lucy, who teaches second grade. Recent work has approached the subject of gender differences from new angles. Sociologist Barrie Thorne, in her book *Gender Play: Girls and Boys in School* (1993), discusses various assumptions about the reasons for gender differences. A developmental view sees such differences as naturally unfolding. A socialization view sees society, role models, school, and the media all socializing children to their proper roles. Thorne's observations in school led her to emphasize another powerful factor: Children actively participate in their own socialization, taking up or resisting the gender possibilities that are perceptible to them.

One afternoon in Lucy's classroom a discussion of a student-authored book led to a debate about "boys' writing" and "girls' writing." The children expressed, shared, and refuted some entrenched ideas about how writing might differ along gender lines and also about gendered interests and knowledge. The discussion showed the children resisting and reforming their own ideas of gender differences.

Bronwyn Davies's book *Shards of Glass: Children Reading and Writing beyond Gendered Identities* (1993) is based on her research with children in Australia. She notes "how subtle, how invisible, how pervasive, and *how much our own* are the discursive mechanisms through which we have come to know our place and remain within it" (8, her italics). Her research aimed at "speaking into being" different ways of living in the world by helping students identify the discourses around them and how these contributed to their sense of themselves. She emphasized children's agency, their active participation as "producers of culture, as writers and readers who make themselves and are made within the discourses available to them" (2). Thus through her work in schools, she sought to move beyond the male-female dualism by opening up possibilities for both boys and girls.

The brief descriptions above illustrate feminism's "refusal to stop changing." All of these questions raised by feminism will come up in the case studies that follow. The broad range of questions is sometimes broken up and labeled as different kinds of feminism. Liberal feminism is most associated with issues of stereotyping, equality, and access; cultural feminism, with a stress on women's values, strengths, history, and community; standpoint feminism, Black feminism, and lesbian feminism, with an insistence on how gender, race, class, sexuality, and other aspects of our individual selves influence how we perceive the world; socialist feminism, with societal pressures, the struggle of individual consciousness, and the possibilities for social change; and postmodern feminism, with a deconstruction of old paradigms and a focus on the power of discourse in shaping our lives and thoughts. The questions brought forward in the earlier days of the Women's Movement, I feel, are no less valid than more recent concerns, and they can hardly be viewed as taken care of. But they are not merely additive either. Rather, the later questions need to be cycled back in taking another look at earlier issues—as this study will attempt to do.

I found that none of the case study teachers could be identified with a single group of concerns—nor did it seem productive to label them. Instead, their concerns overlapped and moved beyond these categories. They changed from day to day and were influenced by their colleagues, the children in their classes, the subject matter, and the circumstances of their professional and personal lives.

Life in schools is profoundly influenced by what we expect of boys and girls, what we think is man's or woman's place on this planet, what we believe is the basis for differences between the sexes, and what power we think holds these distinctions in place. Often we are not entirely conscious of these beliefs and their implications, though they influence our practice nevertheless. Both as a teacher and a researcher I sometimes noticed—or it was pointed out to me—that my actions or my words implied underlying ideas of which I was not sufficiently aware. One function of theory, such as feminist theory, is to help us see how our actions are related to our thoughts and to help us develop a more conscious practice.

In such an ordinary, everyday context as a classroom we need the help of theory so that we can see through constructions of knowledge and relationship that keep us all in our places and have been made to appear so natural that we don't even think about it. In a school greeting song of my childhood, we started the day reminding ourselves that "We're all in our places/With sunshiny faces." I hope in this study to raise questions about those places.

TEACHER AND RESEARCHER

As an elementary school teacher, I often wished I could stop the clock and slow the rotation of the earth so that I could absorb, examine, react to, and maybe understand more of what was happening in my classroom. There was always too much going on—too many needs, too much stuff accumulating on my desk, too many things to stop and appreciate, too many items to follow up on, and often not quite enough energy to give back what I would have liked. This is an underlying reality of a classroom with, say, twenty-four children.

As a researcher, I found it exciting to be somewhat in the position of clock-stopper. I spent my day observing in the classroom, able to move around, pursue what looked interesting, question the students and the teacher, and use audiotape and videotape for later reflection. Then when I went home, rather than correcting papers and planning tomorrow's lessons, I could contemplate the day, type and analyze my notes, and think of questions arising from the day's experience that I wanted to ask at the next opportunity. I found this a rich, luxurious, and productive time. It's the kind of reflective time I wish all teachers could have built into their weekly schedules.

My clock-stopping has taken the form of a qualitative approach to gathering and analyzing data from the classrooms of three feminist elementary school teachers. I wanted to use a research design that would foreground the voices, experiences, and insights of teachers, because I was aware—both from reading and from my own experience—that other people often speak *for* teachers, while teachers rarely get to speak for themselves. Since I was interested not only in the teachers' feminist ideas but in how those ideas played out in practice, I needed to become an observer in the classroom as well as an interviewer of the teachers. My years of experience in elementary schools have given me a deep interest and a sense of comfort in the classroom. I felt this would be an advantage for me as an interviewer and a participant observer—though it was not an unproblematic one, as I will show.

These considerations also led me to choose a case study approach so that I could present a small number of teachers more fully and analyze the data more thoroughly. I included teachers with different feminist and educational ideas, who worked in different kinds of schools, and who handled classroom situations in different ways. My focus was on the details of incidents, the interaction between ideas and practice, the angles of perception and interpretation. The variation among the three contexts reveals what some of the basic issues are for teachers and for students, although they are played out differently in the three settings.

I started this study by interviewing several elementary school teachers who called themselves feminists.[3] I found these teachers through referrals from friends and colleagues whom I had told about my project. I asked, "Do you know any feminist elementary school teachers?" Some people—in reference, I suppose, to a prevailing stereotype about elementary school teachers as passive, conventional, and unintellectual—commented that they thought a *feminist* elementary school teacher was a contradiction in terms. The teachers in this book will prove them wrong. Other people referred me to teachers in alternative schools or women who were thought of as "very good teachers" or radical in some way. "But," my contact sometimes added, "I don't know if she is really a feminist." One teacher whom I called on a colleague's recommendation said emphatically, "I'm not a feminist!" Some teachers rejected the word out of hand. Rosemary's explanation for this was, "It's because they think it means lesbian—that's why they deny the label."

The confusion about recognizing who is "really a feminist" was indicative of a problem of definition that I knew I would encounter: What is feminism? Who is a feminist? At this stage I wanted to let my informants tell me. If, in the first phone conversation, they identified themselves as feminists, I would ask to interview them.

I considered only classroom teachers (that is, not specialists, like art or music teachers) and only elementary school teachers who were teaching first through fifth grade. These are all grades that I have taught, and I thought my experience would help me understand the teachers' work. I made it clear to the teachers at the outset that I had been an elementary school teacher for eighteen years, assuming that this would help them to trust me and give them reason to expect me to be sympathetic.

Lucy confirmed the significance of my previous experience in our first interview. She spoke of an incident I had just witnessed where she had somewhat angrily taken a drawing book away from a child. She said, "[At the time] I thought, 'Oh, I shouldn't have done that. Now Rosie's crying.' But also, I know that you know too. This is a teaching day. These things happen." This sense of a shared background was particularly important since teachers often feel—and with good reason, as I pointed out in the preface—that outsiders do not understand or appreciate their world.

I looked for teachers who had taught for five years or more. Since I was interested in the interaction of their feminism and their practice, I wanted to find teachers who had had a chance to work out some of that integration and who were willing to talk about it.

Rather than identifying the three teachers from the beginning, I started with one teacher, then considered what might be helpful to look for in a second teacher that would broaden and fill out, as well as challenge, my data collection and beginning analysis. This is the "constant comparative method" for multicase studies discussed by Robert Bogdan and Sari Knopp Biklen (1982, 68). My focus was on what I thought was needed in order to present a fuller, more complex picture of the experience of feminist elementary school teachers. My work with Lucy showed that her positioning as a White, middle-class, heterosexual woman was an important aspect of her life story, her choice of teaching as a career, and her understanding of her work. Realizing this, I sought teachers who had had different life experiences and who would offer different angles on teaching. Rosemary is a lesbian in a profession where lesbians have long been "an invisible presence," as Madika Didi Khayatt subtitles her book on lesbian teachers (1992), but are now beginning to make themselves visible. Marcia is an African American with strong links to the African American community from which most of her students come. The study is richer because the three women involved in it are differently positioned with regard to how they experience their work and what they think is critical in their teaching and their feminism.

The three teachers also represent a range of feminist ideas and teaching styles. They taught different grades. The populations of their classrooms varied greatly, as did the schools where they taught. There was further demographic variation in their locations in an inner city, a suburb, and a large town.

One dimension on which the teachers did not vary much is age. They were all from approximately the same generation—in their late forties and early fifties. My daughter, with the perspective of a younger generation, speculated that it is not coincidental that women in this age range would be more apt to embrace the term *feminism*.

Sarah Lawrence-Lightfoot reflected on the significance of middle age in her choice of subjects for her book *I've Known Rivers* (1994). She appreciated the fact that the people she interviewed were reflective and self-critical, interested both in looking back on their earlier lives and also in looking forward to new challenges. This dual perspective is also discernible in my three case study teachers.

As a former teacher, I hoped to be able to participate in the classroom in some helpful ways that didn't interfere with my research, but I soon realized that this was problematic. On the second full day in Lucy's classroom I stationed myself in the art corner where a messy, noisy project was taking place—scooping out potato halves and planting grass seed in them to make "potato head" creatures. I found myself very involved in helping this group—watching the sharp knife, repeating Lucy's instructions, worrying about whether there would be enough materials if the kids used two halves and sixty toothpicks. Later I decided that allowing myself to be drawn in like this was a mistake as I quickly lost track of what else was going on in the room.

But it was hard to resist the pleasure of helping the kids. Writing time was a particular temptation for me and a needy time for the kids. In Marcia's room I watched tiny Deshi pulling together two chairs—one for her, one for me—so that I could help her word by word with her story. I could identify that appealing trap. On another occasion, when I was suddenly deluged with requests for help, I discovered that I had inadvertently sat in the seat of the recently departed student teacher, making me fair game for help on math and spelling papers.

Shulamit Reinharz, in her book on *Feminist Methods in Social Research,* describes the work of Nancy Shaw, a sociologist who found herself helping out in a delivery room where she had wanted to be a "nonparticipatory observer." She felt she "had no right to stand by while another suffered in front of me, or to write while someone else was doing a job that needed two people" (1992, 61). I felt a similar contradiction. It was hard not to pitch in when I could see a line of kids waiting at the teacher's desk.

Immediately after a session in the classroom, I examined my notes to see what statements or incidents I wanted to discuss with the teacher at the next opportunity. Some of our discussions took place during the course of the school day, when the teacher and I had a chance to talk on the fly or during breaks. This varied in each classroom. It was harder, for instance, in Rosemary's room, where there were always other adults needing her attention. In that case I would make a note of issues that I wanted to bring up in the next interview.

After school I conducted several interviews with each teacher.[4] Three of these were semistructured. They focused on particular themes but were left open-ended so that I could follow the teacher's train of thought. One of these was an oral history interview. Another looked at the possibilities and restrictions of the teacher's role. In addition I held three or four interviews with each teacher that were based on things I had observed in the classroom and wanted more information about. I also had questions that arose from the early stages of my ongoing analysis and from interviews with other teachers.

From my first session it was clear to me that these interviews were going to cover a range of personal and professional, relevant and irrelevant, material. I thought it was important to let the interviews become conversations—and to enjoy them too. I took notes on my reactions and observations. I transcribed the interviews myself, incorporating any questions, observations, or reactions I had.

The three case studies are presented here in the order in which I experienced them. Inevitably—and consciously—my interpretation of the second case study was influenced by what I had learned from the first, and the third was influenced by both the first and the second. Marcia and her classroom, however, are not intended to represent the culminating point, the synthesis of the other two cases. Something circular is more what I have in mind. The three cases are necessarily additive, but as I proceed I frequently refer back to the previous studies, attempting to keep all three before the reader.

The teachers' interpretations, from our ongoing discussions of events, are integrated into the text. I gave each teacher a draft of her chapter to read and comment on, and I incorporated her corrections and suggestions, a practice often associated with feminist approaches to research.

After I had finished collecting most of my data[5] and was analyzing it further and writing it up, I kept making new connections and perceiving new layers of meaning. As I reexamined the transcript of a discussion or connected this statement with that bit of behavior, and again later as I struggled with the interpretations of the teachers themselves and of other readers, I began to see what appeared to be deeper, more revealing levels of interpretation and understanding. This was rewarding, but also troubling because not only had I missed some of these insights at the time, it seemed to me some of them could never have been seen in the "real time" of the classroom.

I had hoped that the process of analyzing my data from the classroom and interviews would be a process of simplification—of breaking down complex incidents so that they would be clearer and more comprehensible. What I found is that the complexity increases exponentially. A "simple" classroom incident does not break down into comprehensible parts. It gathers complexity because of the many ways that it can be seen and interpreted. These diverse interpretations can provide more understanding or perhaps a sense of how something could have been managed differently. The clock-stopper inscribes the incident, analyzes the response, addresses various interpretations, and reflects on the whole in the hope that new understanding can at some point be reinserted into the complexity of the classroom.

The next three chapters are case studies of Lucy, Rosemary, and Marcia. Each chapter contains a life history of the teacher and a description of her classroom. The last part of each chapter presents a number of issues and incidents I encountered in the classroom that related to the many questions of feminism discussed earlier.

An intriguing and ongoing issue in my research was that I was dealing with three different realities—or rather three dynamically different versions of a common setting. In retrospect, the first moments in each setting reveal something of the structure of each class, the teacher's conception of my role, and some early indicators of how the research in each classroom might proceed. Here are glimpses of my first afternoon in each school. In each case, I arrived an hour or two before the end of school for a visit in the classrcom before the interview.

I walked into Lucy's class from the hall. There was no doorway, just some shelves indicating a division. The students in her busy class of second graders were engaged in various activities that spilled out into the hall. At first I could not locate the teacher; she was sitting with a group of children. Lucy got up to greet me and exchange a few words. When some kids came over and asked what I was doing there, Lucy said to me, "I think I'll leave you to answer that" and went on to something else.

I arrived early for my appointment with Rosemary. She was still at lunch with her kids. I examined the hall bulletin boards while I waited. Then Rosemary and her class filed down the hall—Rosemary no taller than some of her fifth graders. I went in with the class, which immediately divided up to work in small groups on a series of skits. Rosemary sat with me at a table at the side of the room, explaining what was going on and telling me more about her kids, already interpreting and analyzing.

In Marcia's school I waited in the office for Larry, an envoy from her class, to come and lead me through the maze to her room. Marcia was just coming out of her room with her students, who were on their way to art. I followed Marcia around the school on a tour—not for my benefit, but for an elderly neighbor who had come in to give some oral history in another class. Then Marcia took me along to a meeting with the five other teachers on her team. Finally, we returned to her classroom where the children, returning from art, eagerly took up a variety of activities without a word from their teacher. I sat down with my notebook.

NOTES

1. All the names of students, teachers, and schools used in this book are pseudonyms with one exception. Rosemary Trowbridge insisted that I use her real name. In response to a draft of an earlier article where I had used a pseudonym, she complained, "You're putting me back in the closet!"

2. All terms referring to race are problematic and political. I have tried to use such terms carefully. I use the terms preferred by my informants, authors, or teachers: Patricia Hill Collins writes of *Black Feminism* (1991); Marcia spoke of *African Americans*. I use *women of color* when referring to a broader group.

3. See appendix A.

4. The guides for the interviews mentioned in this paragraph are in appendix B.

5. More information on data collection can be found in appendix C.

2

Lucy: A Search for Self-Definition

If we do not define ourselves for ourselves, we will be defined by others.

—Audre Lorde

I don't want to have a girls' side and a boys' side.

—Rosie

When I entered Lucy's classroom to begin my first case study, I was not prepared for the way I was swept right into the scene—like a character in one of those children's stories, *Mary Poppins*, for instance. You are standing in a room, looking at a picture, when suddenly you find yourself pulled from that observer perspective and plunked into the middle of the picture itself, actually living it. Later, when you have returned to "real" life, you wonder if it all really happened. Then you look back and see how you have created some minute change in the picture—your scarf flew off as you ran across the field, and there it is, a splotch of red that proves you really were there.

Lucy's classroom, however, was no children's story. It was a real life drama of our own time. Lively and diverse, the kids brought in, along with their snacks and homework folders, a broad range of cultural differences, social disparities, and individual issues.

In this context, I imagined myself as a *participant observer,* a term that is something of an oxymoron, because there is a great deal of tension between the roles of observer and participant. From the beginning I relished the opportunity to be an observer of scenes in which I had for years been an actor. But I also wanted to feel part of what was going on in the class-room. I missed being in school and sometimes felt rather more like a teacher than a researcher. I knew my relationship with Lucy would be im-portant to the research; so was my relationship with the children. I wor-ried about them. I rejoiced when things went well. I found I wanted them to like me. It seemed too easy to step into a teacher role. At different times I caught myself scolding Karl, comforting Tracy, and chiding Brianna.

I was also drawn into this scene by the similarities I perceived between Lucy and me as teachers: She had never expected to teach but had been drawn into it after her children were in school. She had taught in a small town, and like me she found she had a lot to learn when she encountered the multicultural classrooms of this city. Her classroom was informal, busy, and varied, reminding me of the way I ran my own class. She put great emphasis on writing and publishing children's writing. She was very interested in feminist issues. Many of these similarities also reflect—in ways that were not sufficiently clear to me at the time but became clearer as my research moved on into other settings—our similar posi-tioning as White, middle-class, heterosexual teachers.

Our positioning was not obvious to us because of the many ways our language, conventions, and school customs assume without saying so that teachers are White, middle class, and heterosexual. These unre-marked positionings are inherently privileged in schools, but that was also hard for us to recognize. As feminists, we tended to see the school system as patriarchal and more or less inimical to women teachers. That made it harder to see how we were implicated in an institution that was also White and middle class, and how we benefited because of who we were. For another thing, we saw our teaching as oppositional. We had both had to fight to do things our way in the classroom and had to resist the sometimes mundane, sometimes major repressions of the system. In other words, we did not identify with the system, which nevertheless privileged us.

Early in the first interview, Lucy and I discovered that we had both been hired as inexperienced teachers with the expectation that our pro-gressive ideas (overlooking our nonexistent experience) would help in-fluence more traditional colleagues. We talked about how miserably we had failed at this and how we had suffered. "This felt like real sharing," I noted in my commentary on the transcript. In the same conversation we discussed how exhausting teaching is. There is a large and profound sigh on the tape, but—listening to it later—I couldn't tell whose sigh it was.

From the beginning Lucy was frank and willing to discuss what was going on in her classroom. She struck me as someone who was used to an-alyzing and questioning and who would be a great asset to my inquiry. She was willing to get involved and helpful in planning the details of my visits—parking, lunch, introductions. Her suggestion on my first full day in class that we go out for lunch to a falafel place near the school delighted me. If the kids had gym just before lunch, Lucy sometimes had time to go out for lunch—albeit at 10:30 A.M. I found her responses encouraging—making me feel welcome, a colleague, rather than an intruder.

These qualities seemed promising for developing the kind of researcher/informant relationship that I had in mind. I imagined a collaborative relationship, one of give-and-take in which I would be the researcher but also a former teacher, and Lucy would be the informant but one interested in the same issues and certainly not just a passive source of information. Lucy also seemed to see the teacher/researcher relationship as one of give-and-take. In the first interview she told me something about her own children, Lesley and Hal, then asked me about mine. Although I had completed several preliminary interviews at that point, this was the first time anyone had asked me a question about myself. Later, after another interview I asked Lucy the de rigueur question, Do you have any questions for me? "No," she said, "I'll interview you—when we're finished, but not today"—and later on she did.

One spring day it was 84 degrees in Lucy's classroom. It had been a tough day, and at the end Lucy and I were both beat. Lucy sat at her desk, which she rarely did, and said, "I haven't read the two articles you gave me yet. I haven't had time. I always have so many things to do, and some just get to the bottom of the list. I've started both of them. I keep wondering, Is this the story of my life—to go home exhausted every afternoon? I have so many good ideas about what I'm going to do in the afternoon—then I'm just too tired."

That day Lucy had to go on to a meeting that she wasn't looking forward to. She said, "I just feel like crying." I felt such empathy with her at that moment, remembering times I'd felt like that as a teacher. Also, I was concerned that this project—and the questioning and reexamining it involved—must be hard on her.

I felt concern about the added burden of my project with all three teachers, but perhaps most immediately with Lucy, because she was in the middle of a very difficult year. She told me at the end of my first day in her classroom that her group was known among members of the faculty as "the class from hell." By the luck of the draw, teachers sometimes have a combination of kids that would be tough by any standards. The range of differences might be taken into account, and the serious individual problems of some of the children might be known in advance, but the way they interact, the way the group as a whole pans out can't always be predicted. Like Lucy, like most teachers, I have had such classes that seem to create a sense of struggle that underlies the whole school year. I visited Lucy's class during subsequent years as well, and found a very different reality, but the year I did most of my research was an embattled year—the kind of year that makes for agonizing reappraisal and leaves one open to feelings of failure.

In the oral history section that follows, I interpret Lucy's story as a search for self-definition. Some of her comments throughout the interviews indicate how she was also striving to define herself against my assumptions and (mis)interpretations as a researcher. After the biographical section I describe Lucy's classroom and then discuss the feminist issues that I found being worked out there.

LUCY'S STORY

In some ways, the "Lucy" inscribed in this part is a character Lucy and I created together, or coconstructed. I have tried to show this by including chunks of transcript that illustrate how my responses reinforced, diverted, or undermined her train of thought and by commenting on what I consider to be my influence on what she chose to include in this conversation. I had created a frame for the interview with the questions I came with—questions about Lucy's own experiences as a girl in school, about her decision to become a teacher, and about the origins of her feminism.[1] I wanted to know this background as part of who she was as a feminist teacher—how had she formed her feminist ideas, and how did they relate to her practice in school? It was within this frame that Lucy talked about herself as a student and teacher, and the frame, therefore, affected the way she interpreted the decisions she made and the way she connected different experiences in her life.

Teaching had been held out to both of us as one of the few available—and one of the most accessible—occupations open to middle-class women. In Lucy's case it was a particularly present possibility because she had aunts—no fewer than three of them—who were teachers. Yet she had not considered teaching as she was growing up. Lucy was emphatic, "I never dreamed I'd be a teacher. Heaven forbid! at the time is what I felt, [laughter] but *they get you in the end!*"

At the beginning of our first interview, Lucy mentioned her daughter Lesley who had stopped by briefly during the school day. She said that Lesley "just lights my day up!" At the time I did not realize how Lesley is intimately connected with Lucy's feminism and her hopes for her girl students, but she became an important, implicit theme in the interview. Lesley is not an intrusion on Lucy's work life; rather, she is inseparable from that life. As Marjorie DeVault (1990) observed in connection with her work on women and meal preparation, there is a blurring of the public and the private, job and home, which she sees as typical of women and "women's work" and not adequately reflected in the language we have to use to talk about these matters. In her book on women and teaching titled *Bitter Milk*, Madeleine Grumet also mentions the contradictions and overlaps between teaching and mothering and how teaching "wedges itself into our lives" in ways that make it hard to draw lines between home and work (1988, xi). Lucy extends this connection between mothering and teaching. She says later on, "It's almost as if I'm the mother of all these kids."

In what follows, the beginning of the life history interview, it is interesting that I had not yet asked Lucy for her perceptions of herself as a girl (which was to be a later question), but simply for her perception of herself as a student. It is hardly possible, however, to think of school in other than gendered terms:

> *Lucy:* I hated school. I was uncomfortable at school. I think of myself as shy?[2] I think I was shy. I wanted to be a good girl. I didn't ever want the teacher to yell at me, so I ascertained what people did to get themselves yelled at, and that was something that I was sure to stay clear of. I listened carefully so that I wouldn't get yelled at, and I did well, but I didn't like it.
>
> *Carla:* Did you *feel* that you did well?
>
> *Lucy:* No, I don't think so. In retrospect, my third grade teacher—we had four marking periods, and she carefully gave me all Cs one term, all Bs the next, and all As the final term. Even as a child I thought, "She's manipulative. She did that just to make herself look good—like she brought me from an average student to an excellent student?" It didn't make sense to me, even as a child. I had pretty strict teachers.

Here at the beginning of the interview, Lucy has already set up the poles between which she strings much of the story of her life in school and beyond: the difference between "being good" and "getting yelled at," which she wants to avoid. She remembers struggling with her own suspicious view of her teacher. This memory, with the thought of her strict teachers, brings up another incident, so that she gives my next question a quick reply and plunges on:

> *Carla:* Now where was this?
>
> *Lucy:* Fairfield.
>
> *Carla:* Fairfield, that's not far.
>
> *Lucy:* No, it's not. In fifth and sixth grade I was in an advanced class that was split into a double grade, and every morning the teacher would put a brainteaser on the chalkboard, and, I hated them. I absolutely hated them! I'm sure that's where math anxiety first developed for me. They were all math brainteasers—word problems.

In the above passage Lucy did not make an explicit connection between the story of her math phobia and being a girl, though it is suggested by the context.

> *Carla:* So you developed a math phobia?
> *Lucy:* Yeah, but I remember now in fourth grade I had it too. I remember in fourth grade I hated the weekend because I could *gruel* myself through the week, but once I got to the weekend it made Monday worse? So I hated the weekends because it meant I had to deal with Monday, which seemed really hard to me. And that was over math too. I don't remember the specifics. I think we might have taken times tests or something which I dreaded and hated. But in fifth grade these word problems really had me in a tizzy. I just felt nauseous before school—every day.

She continued with another math phobia story. Despite her agony over word problems, she also had ability in math; but this ability, rather than giving her a sense of achievement, only got her into trouble. It caused "the worst thing that happened":

> *Lucy:* But *the worst thing* that happened was that we were given standardized tests, and after the standardized tests, the teacher called my parents in to tell them that I had done better than anyone in the town on those tests in word problems, so she was sure I was being stubborn and *willful* about not doing well on them in school. And I never could figure out the discrepancy myself.

Here and elsewhere Lucy uses words in an original way. *Grueling* is one of those words that we use only in particular forms—*grueling* but not ordinarily *to gruel* (like *unkempt*, where we don't use *kempt*). Lucy apparently uses *gruel* to mean *force herself to endure*. She describes herself as *willful*, which is a somewhat old-fashioned word. Perhaps this is the very adjective her teacher once used for her.

Later when I asked about the messages she received about what it meant to be a girl as she was growing up, Lucy hesitated, repeated my question, then remembered a story about her cousin that had great significance for her:

> *Lucy:* Oh, I do remember, hmm, what messages? When I was eleven years old, I had a cousin who was my age—and a boy—who I spent the summer with, and he wanted to commit me to doing something mischievous, and he said, *"The worse thing that could happen* would be we'd get into trouble." And I had never looked at life that way before! And I thought that was worth thinking about and I—it changed my life, really.
> *Carla:* Oh, that's great! I wish that had happened to me. [laughter] I always thought the worse thing was getting into trouble and that *was* the worse thing! [more laughter]

Lucy: I thought that, too, Carla. I mean, I didn't want to get yelled at, but somehow he turned that around for me, the way he worded that or the way he led his life. I thought he was having fun and that was there for me too, if I was willing to just accept the fact that the only bad thing that could happen would be that I'd get into trouble. And we didn't come from the kind of families where we'd ever be hit or anything, so there wasn't any really big threat in the wind.

Lucy, looking back, remembers a part of herself that was restive, not content with staying in her "place." She found new possibilities for her life after facing "the worst thing that could happen." She presents herself as very aware of what was expected of her, aware of the double standard for girls and boys, and aware even then that she could resist that inequity and find ways around the double standard.

I felt a lot of empathy with Lucy throughout this section of the interview. Perhaps it is because I was so connected with her memories that I had a sudden recollection of an almost forgotten summer, which I jotted down in my field notes. I didn't see what the connection was until later:

When she told this story, I flashed on that summer at Aunt Ruth's and the neighbor boy I made friends with. Funny, because at the moment I thought the connection was just friendship with a boy. Later, typing this up, I remembered the one vivid picture I have of that summer: a shady swimming hole with an old cement dam covered in moss, slippery with a slight stream of water flowing over it. The boy and I were having a great time sliding down it. I remember longing to go on and enjoy it but worrying and stopping, because I discovered I was wearing a hole in the seat of my bathing suit.

What would have happened? What would have been "the worse thing that could happen?" Probably, I would have been called careless for ruining the bathing suit.

The connection I recovered later was the conflict between our own pleasure (associated with mischief or trouble) and a guilty, internalized sense of what was supposed to be right (for girls who didn't want to get yelled at). In our conversation, Lucy and I followed this theme a little longer before she made it clear that she didn't want to go any further:

Carla: So, did you get into trouble?
Lucy: I don't think we did. We did lots of things, and we didn't even get into trouble, because we were careful.
Carla: So what happened after that summer?
Lucy: I did more mischievous things after that. I wouldn't care to elaborate . . . but I learned to be a bad girl, you know, for a while.
Carla: Really? In school, too?
Lucy: I don't think I was. No, I don't think I was so bad in school. And it wasn't even at home. It was more subversive.

I felt I had to respect her setting of boundaries, and I backed off, though I found her hints tantalizing. "A bad girl," I think, has to be understood in the context of Lucy's life. Whatever badness she got into, she had some middle-class buffers. Her badness did not prevent her from following the prescribed 1950s script of going to college, getting married, and having children.

In an effort, perhaps, to move away from her own getting into trouble, Lucy then generalized this issue and made it more abstract. She associated the theme of not wanting to get into trouble with a desire for connection and the theme of getting into trouble with independence.

> *Carla:* But you think of that [being a bad girl] as a positive development?
> *Lucy:* Yeah, I think it relates to, um, this really basic oversimplified view of gender differences that I refuse to let go of: that women basically want to connect and men basically want to be independent. And if you want to connect, you don't want disapproval. And if you don't want disapproval, then you don't want to get into trouble. But if you want to be independent, you don't mind getting into trouble, and you don't mind bucking authority. That shows your independence.

The contrast Lucy perceives is developed by Bronwyn Davies, whose work concerns the construction of masculinity and femininity in childhood. Davies points out that for boys who are pursuing "their own heroic narratives, . . . [a]n adult reprimand is a signal of their correct placement in the heroic storyline that they are playing out (usually) to their audience of peers," whereas girls tend to experience "anger and deep shame if their actions are defined by adults as transgressive" (Davies 1993, 92).

A connection between these experiences of Lucy's as a girl and her beliefs as a teacher is implied in the following passage. The connection she wants to make, though, is not an easy one, as reflected in her hesitancy and self-interruption.

> *Carla:* So what about the mischievous, unruly side and the connecting-with-people side? Do you think those are both parts of you?
> *Lucy:* I think they are, but the connecting side is much stronger. And it's certainly true as a teacher, that I would like the girls to be—I want them to be—on the one hand—I mean, I don't want an unruly class. But I'd like the girls to take enough risks, and I'd like the boys to have more consideration for others, and connection.
> *Carla:* Oh, wow, what a project that is. Who are some of the girls that you think—
> *Lucy:* Tracy.
> *Carla:* Yup, I heard Tracy say, "Make me!" to Reggie. I thought, "I hope he doesn't take her up on it."

There was another girl in the class, Rosie, who was a trial to Lucy. She saw her as belligerent, always "sticking her jaw out." Both she and Tracy, in other words, had attitude. They represent some of the dimensions of the issue of what a girl can/should be like. Part of the complication for Lucy is that here she is in the position of authority. She is the one doing the "yelling," and, of course, she does not want an unruly class.

In the next passage, the use of the word *askew* is notable, both because it is an unusual word and because it captures so effectively the contradiction, the sense of something *willful* or *unruly*, in Lucy's memories of herself and her conflicting hopes for other girls, like Tracy:

> *Lucy:* At a parent conference I gave Tracy's mother a cartoon in which a little girl was standing *askew*, with hair askew and clothes askew and she said, "I'm independent, explora—?" What would you use? "I like to explore. I'm curious and independent. I'm outspoken," and other such adjectives. And then at the bottom it says, "Needless to say, I don't have many friends." And that's really the story of Tracy—because she is all those things.

Elsewhere Lucy refers to Tracy as a "speak-your-own-mind girl" and a "feminist in the making."

After the discussion of badness, the conversation returned to Lucy's discrepant math performance. That anomaly, and its attendant problems, continued to haunt her:

> *Lucy:* Almost the identical thing happened in my freshman year of high school. On the last day of class, I remember my algebra teacher saying, "OH!"—he was announcing the standardized test results—and he said [sarcastic], "And even Miss Dudley was in the 99th percentile!" And then all the bad boys laughed. I don't know why, but they teased me.
>
> *Carla:* Did they tease you about doing well in math, or about *not* doing well?
>
> *Lucy:* I don't know! Both, I think, but I don't know. I'm sure I did my assignments, but I must have been perceived as a person who could take kidding and would take kidding. But it didn't feel so good inside.
>
> *Carla:* So you did well, you got good grades?
>
> *Lucy:* Yeah, but they weren't super great. When I was a junior I remember the math teacher sending an announcement of a state competition down to the art room where I always hung out, and my friends just cracking up at the thought of me competing in a state math competition. My best friend at the time was a boy who was an art student too, and he was very, very much like Woody Allen. We spent all of our time together—most of my high school years. And his jokes were endless over that. He just thought that was hilarious. And I was embarrassed, because it didn't fit with my self-image.

In these stories Lucy reflects on the role of math in her school experiences. To a great extent, our society views math as male. Males do better on math achievement tests and are more likely than girls to major in math in college and go on to careers that require math (American Association of University Women 1992). Lucy herself in looking back sees a certain awkwardness and inappropriateness in her math ability. It seemed inappropriate—hilarious—to her boyfriend as well. There is an implicit association of math with maleness and with badness: Math gets her into trouble.

In contrast, Lucy's image of herself was as an artist. After high school she went to college at an art school in the city where her three teacher-aunts lived. Lucy recalled a significant development during those years:

> *Lucy:* Oh! You know what? That's the most interesting part of the story, actually. I lived with my spinster aunts for three years when I went to college, but the year *before* that—my first year of college—I lived with an aunt who was married. She was the mother of the cousin who taught me how to, um, *reexamine* my concepts of getting in trouble, so I lived with her.
>
> She had become a teacher, in much the same way I have. She had been an English major. After her kids had grown up, she needed to do something else and had fallen into teaching. She was a captivating, you know, a really gifted teacher. And every night during my freshman year we'd do the dishes together, and she would recount her day. She's very much of a storyteller. I'm sure she embellished those stories. She always had herself as an incredible *heroine*, but her stories were wonderful. And she had a teacher who was a villain and horrible to kids and the stories of all the kids and the things that went on in her classroom—and I loved them!

In her book *School Work: Gender and the Cultural Construction of Teaching,* Sari Knopp Biklen (1995) discusses the possibilities of the heroic teacher in connection with certain contemporary films in which such a figure is usually male. The heroic is contrasted to the domestic. Gendered interpretations of the concept of hero, Biklen writes, give us male heroes who "are active and accomplish something," versus females who "are able to accept and survive harsh realities" (Biklen, 3). Lucy's aunt, however, disrupts the stereotype by casting herself as a heroic teacher who accomplishes things.

Lucy heard these tales of the heroic teacher over the dishes, which still made up a good portion of the heroine's life. At that time the stories did not make Lucy want to become a teacher. She was bent on that other career that was held out to middle-class women of her generation: marriage and a family. Despite the fact that "women *did* things" in her family, she had no expectation that she would have to support herself.

> *Lucy:* Even though I found her stories fascinating, I didn't personalize it to, "Gee, this is what I want to do." I still thought, "What I want to do is find

someone who will support me in style and let me stay home for the rest of my life." That's what I thought I was going to do. I don't think I would ever have admitted that at the time. The reason I say "admitted" is, I came from a family in which the women *did* things. They were teachers. They were all teachers.

On another occasion:

> *Lucy:* No, I think I wanted to do that awfully stupid thing of getting married and having children. And I thought that that would be a way of doing my art? If I got married and had children I could kind of retreat from the work world and just live in a fantasy kind of world and be an artist. But it didn't work out that way at all.

Lucy's dream for herself, the dream that "didn't work out at all," occupied the minds of many middle-class women at the time, even those with a college education. Lucy imagined herself in a home embellished by fantasy, art, and children. She would not have to work outside the home. The year after she graduated from college, however, Lucy started teaching art in elementary school.

> *Lucy:* I got a job teaching art because I had graduated with an art degree. My future husband was a year behind me in college. So I went up there and actually got a job fresh out of college. But it was back in those days when you could do things like that. I got a job teaching art in a school system that had never had an art teacher before in the elementary grades. And this is so stupid—I, being as forthcoming as I am, didn't try to hide the fact that Ron and I were living together. And it was too soon for that. The elementary supervisor called me in to her office and shut the door and said, "What do you think your mother would say?" I said, "My mother knows! She would say, you know, 'Do what you need to do with your life.'"[laughing] My mother was pretty good, you know. I mean, she wouldn't condone it. I wouldn't put her on that level, but she also trusted me to do what I thought was right. So after that they gave me such a hard time—I mean they just picked at me—and actually edged me out.
> *Carla:* Who? The administration? The other teachers?
> *Lucy:* No, the administration. I didn't get to know the teachers. I had an incredible job—that was the other thing. I had to travel around to all these different schools. I started with the upper elementary schools. I had discipline problems, but I thought I was up to it. And the administration didn't even know what they wanted, so they'd pull apart my lessons. They'd call me in at the end of each week to see what I'd done, and I'd tell them about it, and they'd say, "We don't think much of this." And they would pick it apart. And I couldn't stand it. I didn't have the *stamina!*[3] [laughing]
> *Carla:* You could take it from the kids but not the—
> *Lucy:* I couldn't take it.

Lucy's description makes a vivid picture of an impossible job. Completely isolated from the other teachers, she runs from school to school giving different groups of students short art lessons, which must surely have been largely devoted to housekeeping chores like handing out supplies and cleaning up afterward. Not only is she trying to do a job that requires superhuman *stamina*, she is also under suspicion for "bad" behavior.

> *Lucy:* I couldn't take it, so I quit, after two months. And then I went back to the city where my aunts lived, and I substitute taught there. I loved it— absolutely loved it. I taught kindergarten through sixth grade, and I just, I would just feel like when I walked into a school, *I would just come alive*. And I *loved* being with these different classes, and I found the kids fascinating.

Here Lucy uses a powerful image for what teaching means to her—the feeling of coming alive in the classroom. This phrase suggests energy, growth, and creativity, the basis of her love of teaching.

While Lucy was substituting, she was sometimes sent to the school where one of her aunts taught. "So I would get to see her in person, and she would see me in person, and it was fun." At the end of that year she married Ron—not quite the romanticized dream that she mentioned earlier, but a decision influenced by economic necessity, conventional mores, and the Vietnam War.

> *Lucy:* Then we both got jobs teaching. We decided we'd have to get married, because we weren't going to go through that again. Then, there was Vietnam. He had a, I don't know, it was a high or low draft number, but he joined the Air Force, and I got pregnant. Kind of classic story. After that, I didn't go back to teaching for ten years, and I didn't have any credentials.

Lucy followed her husband west, where he was stationed. During this time, while her two children, Lesley and Hal, were little and Ron was in the Air Force, Lucy took courses and got certified to teach, though she didn't start teaching until later. In preparing for teaching, she seemed to be following the advice of one of her aunts:

> *Lucy:* I remember having a conversation with her when my kids were babies. We were talking about what I would do with my life, and I said, "I'm really not sure I want to be a teacher." And she said, "But you know what, you can always teach until you decide what you do want to do." And I think she may have just said that helping me to do it, whether or not I needed to do it for life was unimportant at that moment. It was something to do.

Here Lucy's aunt hits the theme of the temporary and contingent nature of teaching as a job for women. For some White, middle-class women teaching, particularly elementary school teaching, has long been seen as "something to do," a stopgap, rather than a serious career commitment.

Later, Lucy and Ron moved again. Lucy was still at home with the children, but as she says in the following quote, something must have been "brewing," which led to the experience that she associates with the beginning of her feminism. Her daughter Lesley, the older child, was in second grade, when Lucy noticed her basal reader:

> *Lucy:* When my daughter was in second grade, I very casually looked through her basal reader. It was 1977 or 1978, I think, and I was absolutely appalled. [school loudspeaker] I did an informal inventory of how many stories had female characters as their heroines and how many had males, and I found that only one story in this entire thick basal had a little girl playing the main character as the heroine, and her heroine-ism was based on [ironic voice] *turning the other cheek*, being a good girl and not speaking up when she was being taken advantage of, and *I—was—furious!*
>
> Now, of course, there had to be a lot brewing or I wouldn't have responded that way. It wasn't only that one moment, but that just set off a whole lot of other emotions. In contrast, I remember one particular story—but there were others—in which the little boy who was the hero had the role of putting his finger in the dam. I don't think that's actually what it was, but it was something that even adults wouldn't do. I mean, he took on an enormous heroic role, and the contrast was too much for me.

Lucy was furious not only because of the gross disparity in numbers of male and female main characters, but also because of the completely different definitions of heroism, in which boys are portrayed as powerful and girls are set up to be taken advantage of.

Soon after this episode, Lucy started to teach kindergarten. She taught for two years in a small town. During this same time, her marriage broke up. The rather stark picture Lucy gives of her marriage strikes again the theme of conformity, of trying to be "good," to revise oneself to fit an ideal or the rules or someone else's expectations.

> *Lucy:* My first husband was a very jealous man, a very insecure, possessive man. When I married him he was very handsome and very intelligent, you know, and I didn't think that much else mattered. I remember reading Carl Rogers during my first marriage, reading a case history, and I couldn't believe it that someone else had actually felt like I had. This woman talked about the man she had married. It sounded very much like the way she [sic] felt about my first husband. She had thought the fact that she didn't love him or that they weren't necessarily compatible was unimportant and that she had to *be someone other than who she was* in order to be in the marriage.

Given such expectations, Lucy saw her divorce as a liberating experience:

> *Lucy:* I left my first marriage, so when I did that I really got my voice back
> and my self back, which I felt had been constrained and restrained during the
> space of my first marriage, which was thirteen years.
>   I felt very free, very free. You know, as I said, there was no big change. I
> just, I didn't have to always, I always deferred to him ultimately, because it
> wasn't worth the hassle of arguing about anything, just about.

Some years later Lucy married again—a man she sees as quite the opposite of her first husband—and moved from a small town to a large city,
where she found her current job.
   I asked her if her feminist ideas had changed since that original moment of looking through her daughter's textbook.

> *Lucy:* No, they've just gotten stronger. I mean, the biggest proof of my fem-
> inist ideas—as is probably true for you, too—is my daughter. She is so aware
> of any gender bias and able to deal with it head-on, without getting too emo-
> tional about it. Oh, she gets pretty emotional, too. She's written some good
> articles for the school paper, and I think—I feel like she's very assertive. She's
> my fantasy of what I, what I could have been, not what I could have been,
> but I feel like I really trained her to—
> *Carla:* You're pleased.
> *Lucy:* Yeah, I'm very pleased.

So Lucy returned to the subject of her daughter, where we started the
conversation. She seemed unambiguous about her daughter as the
"biggest proof" of her feminist ideas and hints, although she pulled back
from the idea that she wished she were more like her.
   The situation in her classroom, however, is ambiguous and contradictory. Because this year she has such a difficult class, her time and energy
are drained away by discipline issues. In this context, she sees the girls as
sometimes having to endure, to "gruel" their way through school—as she
had to do. She wants to help them but feels it is only the "already forth-
right, speak-your-own-mind girls" in second grade who are able to hold
their own against the freer, more outspoken boys. "After a day like this,"
she said once, she worries that what she does as a feminist teacher is "not
that different," not just what she would want it to be.
   A theme in Lucy's experience that also seems relevant to her girl students is the sense of a struggle to find one's way between opposite poles
of patient endurance and "askewness," of passively accepting the structure and role prescriptions of society and school or actively resisting
them, of being defined by others or defining ourselves. This theme res-
onated with me and seemed to echo back a century and more to Victorian
definitions of True Womanhood and the self-definition struggles of actual

women who were then, in increasing numbers, taking on the role of schoolteacher.

LUCY'S CLASSROOM

The school where Lucy teaches is in a large suburb. It stands on a broad street, lined with a variety of shops and fast-food restaurants. There are both apartment buildings and private homes with small yards in the immediate neighborhood. Like many schools in growing communities, the rather grand original structure has sprouted wings with the more efficient architecture of the 1950s and 1960s. A playground partially surrounds the school. In pleasant weather, elderly neighbors sometimes stop with their newspapers or shopping bags and rest on the benches along the sidewalk, while they watch the children at play.

The school holds 730 students in kindergarten through eighth grade. Most of the students live nearby and walk to school—alone or escorted by parents or baby-sitters. In the morning some of the parents bring their children right in to Lucy's room and stop for a moment to chat with her or with their children's friends. The only bus students are those who come via a program that buses children from the inner city to suburban schools.

Lucy's second grade classroom is in one of the new wings. It is a large room with space for different kinds of activities: an art area with a sink, a block area, a corner for Legos, a table for chess and other board games, a circle marked with masking tape on the carpet for class meetings. Everywhere there are colorful and attractive books, games, and art materials arranged to be accessible to the children. On the walls are children's art and commercial posters, and an intriguing collage that Lucy made, in which every child appears as an animal that he or she chose. The children's heads, cut from their annual school pictures, are superimposed on the animals' bodies.

On one side of the classroom is a wall of windows with carefully tended geraniums on the sills. There is no wall on the side facing the hallway, although the room's boundaries have been suggested by dividers and shelves. The teacher's desk is in a corner and is used mostly for storage and to collect papers; Lucy rarely sits at it. The children's desks are arranged in small groups of four or five. The variety of materials and the aesthetic sense with which Lucy has arranged it all make this classroom a rich and inviting environment for learning.

Every morning Lucy posts the schedule on the board. The schedule varies with the day of the week, depending mostly, as is often the case in elementary schools, on the schedule of the specialists—the music, gym, art, library, and computer teachers. The specialists must be scheduled for every classroom, which determines the day's schedule and the teachers' precious "preparation time." Here is Lucy's posted schedule for Monday, with some comments from my notes:

Monday

8:00–8:30	The children arrive—not all at once. Lucy says she loves having the kids straggle in; it starts her day off gradually, but she acknowledges it drives some of her colleagues crazy.
8:00–9:00	*Early morning work.* Lucy calls this her "curtain" time (see below). The kids pick up their assignments from bins at the front of the room. One day they had a spelling worksheet, a little child-made notebook of math problems to be solved, and an assignment to make a trading card, which they had started the day before. The assigned work is intended to leave time for the children to socialize, to catch up with each other, and to choose other activities.
9:00	*Math lab.*
10:00	*Snack and meeting time.* The children bring their snacks to the meeting circle and sit on the floor, while they talk about various topics brought up by either Lucy or the students.
10:30	*Gym.*
11:00	*Lunch.*
11:20	*Recess.*
11:45	*Quiet reading.* The children must "be with a book" for this period. Lucy usually meets with small groups or individuals.
12:30	*Writing workshop.*
1:15	*Cleanup.* The children at each group of desks are assigned some specific chores or areas of the room to tidy.
1:30	*Story.* Lucy reads to the class in the meeting circle.
2:00	*Dismissal.* Lucy hands out the homework folders. Many children are picked up by their parents or older siblings; several go on to an after-school program at the school; two children go home by bus.

Although the schedule changed depending on the day of the week, it didn't vary much from week to week. Lucy adhered to the schedule only loosely, often extending or switching activities or adding some free time. "Curtain time" first thing in the morning was a part of the school day that she thought was especially important. In her metaphor, the curtain refers to the ostensible activities—the spelling and math—but what she sees as more significant is what goes on behind that curtain, the psychological and social dynamics of the children. This block of time gives her an opportunity to observe and interact, to catch up with her kids at the beginning of a new school day.

That spring, there were twenty-three children in Lucy's class, twelve girls and eleven boys. The group was racially, linguistically, and culturally diverse. There were two girls from Haiti; a Puerto Rican boy; a boy from India, who had been adopted by White American parents; a boy from Iran; a girl from Bolivia; a girl from Russia; an Israeli girl; a girl whose mother was Spanish and father, Israeli; a Latina girl; two African American children, a boy and a girl, who came by bus from the city; and eleven European American children, whose ethnic backgrounds (for instance a boy whose family was from Ireland) were sometimes mentioned in class. Two of the children were in a transitional bilingual program; several other children in the class were bilingual but did not need the extra program; the girl with the Spanish and Israeli parents was fluent in three languages.

Lucy taught a majority of these children for two years. She had arranged with another teacher to switch assignments every other year, so that they could each have the same group for first and second grades. This arrangement was not school policy, but Lucy's own preference. Only eight of her children were new to her that particular year.

I had known from my second visit that Lucy was dealing with an especially difficult class. Classes are put together in various ways in different schools. In my school the teachers spent a lot of time each spring working out classes for the fall, trying to find creative combinations and to avoid potentially explosive ones. But the results tended to be iffy, and sometimes the interaction in a particular group could add such stress to the ordinary overload of teaching that a teacher might never seem to get on top of it. Even though Lucy knew most of the children, she did not anticipate the effect of this particular combination of kids. The remarkable thing is that Lucy, knowing about this group in January when I first met her, still let me into her room. It speaks for her courage, her openness, and her willingness to learn from a new experience.

It seemed to me that "the class from hell" exaggerated—and possibly illuminated—some profound, underlying issues in this (or any) classroom and thus made visible what might otherwise be invisible in a more placid, contented group of students. Over the next two years, when I went back to Lucy's classroom, I was struck by the contrast: Matters that had been burning issues the year I did my research later seemed hardly a problem at all. For example, in the following pages the block area is described as a site of frequent conflict, but during my visits in subsequent years, it seemed to be merely a happy place to play.

The year I made my observations, the tensions in Lucy's classroom seemed to split along the fault lines of our society—along the lines of gender, class, and race. I will begin my discussion of classroom issues with gender, my primary focus as I began this project and also an issue of great importance to Lucy. I will first discuss questions of fairness, or equity, and then show how prominent the issue of gender differences can be in a classroom as well as how difficult it is for a teacher to be completely fair while dealing with the range of differences the group of children represent. Next I attempt to expand the gender focus by examining incidents that reflect the influence of race and class as well as gender. Finally, in the section called "Power, Teaching, and Mothering," I discuss how Lucy handled these tensions and other discipline issues in the classroom.

Gender and Equity

When I first called Lucy, she told me that she thinks about gender issues *all* the time in her second grade classroom. "The day is full of issues for me that are really linked with gender—with boys and girls." Her explicit and emphatic statement made me think her classroom would be a good one in which to look at girls and boys and to see how a feminist teacher deals with these differences. Her own awareness and the tensions in the class combined to give a picture of gender writ large and to lay out some of the enormous challenges that a teacher faces in attempting to steer a course that treats children fairly and also celebrates their differences.

Lucy said of girls, "I feel they need to be encouraged to be heroines," and she tried to provide such encouragement in her classroom. She wanted to promote girls' participation in class discussions, their excitement about learning, their achievement (particularly in math), and their exposure to positive role models. Her concern for these issues is directly related to her own experiences, both as a child, who felt persecuted for her superior math ability, and as a parent, who was enraged by the negative images of girls she found in her daughter's basal reader.

Lucy looked for strong, positive role models for girls in what they read. When she read out loud to the class at the end of the day, she alternated between stories with heroes and those with heroines. Before my first day of observation, she had been switching between two books of fairy tales, *The Dark Way* and *Woman in the Moon*. She had chosen the latter because she knew it contained stories with female heroines.

The gender implications of these titles were not lost on the kids, as some of the boys started groaning when she said it was time for the *Woman in the Moon*. From it she read "The Nagging Husband," a story in which the husband and wife switch roles for a day, and the husband, who has believed his wife's work to be relatively easy, produces a series of disasters. This story served to emphasize stereotypical male and female roles, as fairy tales often do, although it also, as Lucy pointed out, hinged on the difficulty and importance of "women's work."

In helping her girls to be heroines, Lucy also urged them *not* to fall into more stereotypical roles. On one occasion this meant abandoning an idea she had tried. She had brought in a basket of small pencils and pads for the children in case they wanted to take notes on what someone said in a class discussion. It sounded like a neat idea, and I thought it would make my presence there—with my pad and pen—more natural. Neither of us had foreseen how it would work out, however. Lucy said, "I was *appalled* when I saw only girls taking notes, and then I thought, 'They're like little secretaries, writing down the words of the master, i.e., the boys.'" Because of this unanticipated result, she decided to put the basket of notepads away.

Lucy was aware of the literature that addresses the issue of boys getting more attention in the classroom (American Association of University Women 1992; Sadker and Sadker 1994). She was also aware of the problem from her own experience. "The boys are so loud and so forceful about getting their ideas across. I mean, they're not the least bit shy about voicing their ideas." She tried to balance this effect in various ways. For example, she said that when she asked a math question, she called on more girls than boys. She described a strategy she used in class discussions:

> *Lucy:* I try to focus my attention on the girl that's speaking and ignore the boys. Then sometimes I point out to them, "I didn't hear you because I was listening to Nora." And they're still young enough that mainly they want to tell me what they think. They're not really speaking for the whole audience. They're speaking for my audience.

My interpretation of the same scene, which occurred about an hour after I had first arrived in Lucy's classroom, was a little different. The following excerpt is from my field notes:

> The book was *The King's Equal.* Some of the kids seemed very absorbed in the story. Lucy allowed open comments when she paused in her reading—and even interruptions. The boys were very forthcoming. They made a lot of comparisons with other books they had read—*King Arthur, The Prince and the Pauper.* They clearly dominated the conversation. Lucy tried to balance by listening carefully to the girls and ignoring the boys, who would continue to comment whether or not she was paying attention to them.

Lucy reacted to my use of the word *allowed* when she read this passage. *Encouraged* was more her intention. She loved the children's spontaneous reactions, and she said, "I don't want to have the kind of classroom control where everybody has to be quiet and wait till they're acknowledged."

This is a tough issue for teachers. A classroom where individual freedom is encouraged could be a classroom where some voices get silenced—in this case, the girls. What amount of control—in what different situations—is necessary in order to have fairness? The three case-study teachers had different responses to this problem.

Lucy had read about teachers who, although they were conscious of the problem, were far from granting equal time to the girls in their classes. Even well-known feminist writer Dale Spender (1982) was shocked to discover from a videotape of a class she had taught that the girls, whom she thought she had favored, had in fact talked only 35 percent of the time. Lucy was curious about how her class would stack up, so we agreed that I would do a tally one afternoon during the end-of-school reading in the meeting circle. I kept track of who raised their hands, who spoke out without raising their hands, who got recognized by Lucy, who talked at length, and who was silent (see table 2.1). Nan was absent that day, making the number of girls and boys equal.

Later, when Lucy and I were discussing this session, she asked me, "Weren't Nora's comments fascinating?" I realized I had no idea what Nora said. The business of filling out the tally had taken all my attention.

When I first tallied the responses, I reported to Lucy that she had called on an almost equal number of girls and boys. A closer look, however, showed that the boys spoke out more often and got recognized more frequently when they spoke out. They were also more apt to speak out when they were *not* recognized, more apt to speak at length, and less apt to be silent. In other words, a simple count of the children Lucy called on covers up how much more actively the boys were involved in this discussion.

Table 2.1 Responses during Reading Out Loud

	Girls	*Boys*
Number of students	11	11
Responses recognized by Lucy	12	13
Raising hand	7	2
Speaking out	5	11
Unrecognized responses	4	18
Raising hand	1	1
Speaking out	3	17
Silent	5	3
Speaking at length	0	2
Total responses	16	31

Lucy was concerned about the quality as well as the quantity of the girls' participation. For instance, in what follows, she compares the contributions of various students during another reading out loud session:

> *Lucy:* I think Nora and Tracy make a lot of very insightful comments, but can they balance Harold, Henry, Neil, Larry? I mean, I feel like the boys are more attentive and they're getting more out of those oral readings, which I think are really important. And the stories, I mean the concepts that I'm presenting at that time are things they can't yet read on their own, and they can't process in the same way, so that's the main way of some of those values being transmitted [at that time, she was reading *The Value of Honesty: Confucius*]. So I hear Harold making all these connections. I think he was the one today that said, "Oh, is he, isn't he the one that first taught the Golden Rule?" I thought that was incredible.
>
> *Carla:* Yes, it was. And Vic takes his thumb out of his mouth, and he comes out with these profound statements.
>
> *Lucy:* And meanwhile behind me, Brianna is playing some kind of little teasing game with Dolores. And Debbie and Raina are usually whispering to each other. It's only my already forthright, speak-your-own-mind girls—Tracy and Nora—who are really involved with the discussion. Nan sometimes is.

Some further information on the girls mentioned in this quotation might help in understanding Lucy's comments. Raina and Debbie were inseparable. They looked similar, and to me at first they were practically indistinguishable. They did everything together, always sat together and worked together. They were producing a series of books about themselves and some real and imagined adventures. The series was entitled *The Adventures of R & D*. In the spring of second grade, they were writing *R & D Worry about Third Grade*. Their chief worry, of course, was that they would not be in the same class next year. According to Lucy, Debbie was not only the most popular girl in class, she was the only child who had *never* volunteered to talk in a whole-class meeting in the two years that Lucy had taught her.

Tracy was introduced in the previous section as Lucy's idea of a future feminist, a speak-your-own-mind girl whose strong opinions seemed to make her unpopular and who was not afraid to stand up to the toughest boy in the class.

Nora is the child mentioned in the first chapter who made the observations about language that words like *woman* and *human* are derived from *man*; she wanted more "words for us." She struck me as remarkably mature and empathetic for a second grader. During another reading-aloud session, Nora supported the silent Debbie:

> Lucy shows the picture and asks, "Doesn't it look like he is holding it up?" Nan corrects her, "She is holding it up." Just in front of me, Debbie asks Nora a question. Later Debbie whispers, "She's going to put a rock in his mouth."

Nora raises her hand, tries to tell Lucy—"Debbie thought she was going to put a rock in his mouth."

Nan makes an important correction here, and Nora *almost* gets Debbie to speak, or at least to contribute an idea. At any rate, when I related this scene to Lucy, she thought that was Nora's intention.

Even this small amount of information about a few of the girls in Lucy's second grade suggests how different they are, how differently they present themselves in the classroom, and, therefore, how complex it is to think of providing a learning environment in which every one of them can flourish.

Lucy said she used to feel more sympathetic to boys in general, but has since changed her mind:

> *Lucy:* I used to be quite sympathetic to the fact that, especially in the lower grades, it's very hard on boys to be sedentary, and the lower grades are easier for girls, but I've become much more sympathetic to how it feels to the girls—even though from outward appearances they're successful.
> *Carla:* Wait a sec. I don't think I follow that. You were more sympathetic to boys. You mean more than girls, or more than you are now?
> *Lucy:* I think so. I think I was more sympathetic to boys for many years.
> *Carla:* So now you're saying, you're more sympathetic to girls—the cost to girls of seeming successful?
> *Lucy:* Yeah, I feel like I'm sympathetic to both of them, but if I had to lean one way or the other, I'd lean toward girls. Because the fact that they can be successful at sedentary tasks doesn't mean they prefer them, or that it brings out their best.

Lucy makes an important point about the problematic aspects of girls' apparent success at sedentary tasks. Her comment recalls her own experiences as a girl in conflict between behaving as she is expected to behave and getting into mischief. She used the weekly music class as an example of what she meant by the cost to girls. The one session I attended with her class was shockingly out of control and painful to sit through. As Lucy was aware, the children dreaded music class, but she felt that the girls suffered more in that class than the boys did.

> *Lucy:* I think, well, I think it's hardest on the girls, because they feel like there's no win. They're stuck there for half an hour in this horrible chaotic situation. It's awful—
> *Carla:* Some of them were trying to follow what Mr. Leonard was doing, but they would, you know, you'd feel like a fool obeying in that class.
> *Lucy:* Isn't it *grueling*?
> *Carla:* I can't tell you how horrible it felt.

In this passage Lucy uses the word *grueling*, which is familiar from her own story, when she had to "gruel herself through the week" in school, dreading it because of the looming word problems. Lucy comes back to music class later, when she refers to it as a "test of endurance," connecting it with *gruel* and *stamina*, words she uses in describing women's experience.

Lucy is aware of how hard it is to foster equity in a classroom situated in an unequal world. There are so many issues, and some of them are easily overlooked, even by those of us for whom they are a matter of concern, making us unwillingly complicit. One day after school both Lucy and I came up against our own complicity. I showed her my sketch of how the kids were sitting in the meeting circle—the girls relatively close, the boys more on the outskirts. Raina and Debbie were not in the circle at all, but on the other side of the divider, scraping off old labels. Lucy said they had asked her earlier why the shelves had the wrong labels. For example one label read tape, but the shelf held paper. She asked if they'd like to change them, and of course they said they would love to. So there they were, two bright but basically nonparticipatory girls, scraping off tape on the other side of a divider, while Lucy led the rest of the class in thinking about Confucian philosophy. When she made this observation, I told her that I had just realized that morning that I had been paying too much attention to the boys in my field notes and therefore was less aware of what the girls were up to. Lucy and I were dismayed at these examples of how we were both unconsciously playing into the very situation we were trying to disrupt.

The effort to be fair—as either a teacher or a researcher—is a challenging and complex one. The task seems made more difficult by the degree to which girls and boys are—or are perceived as being—different.

The Salience of Gender Differences

The children in Lucy's classroom were racially, culturally, and linguistically diverse. In addition, they varied a great deal in maturity, as manifested by their physical size and social skills. The differences and divisions between boys and girls were not obscured by all this diversity, however, and were still powerful influences in the classroom.

Children bring ideas about gender with them into school, where their ideas are challenged and developed on the playground and in the classroom. At times any class can suddenly flair up along gender lines. Teachers have different ways of handling these divisions: quashing them, allowing them, emphasizing them, examining them. At different times, Lucy did all of these things.

Gender arrangements in classrooms are initially revealed by the positioning of the desks. In the classrooms of my childhood, boys and girls sat in rows in an alternating pattern as a means of social control. Today desks are more apt to be arranged in groups. Sometimes the groups are gender mixed, sometimes they are gender divided. Does the teacher make the arrangement or allow the children their free or mediated choice? In this tricky matter, Lucy had come to a compromise:

> *Carla:* Do the girls and boys sit together in their groups?
> *Lucy:* They prefer not to. And that's another issue that I go back and forth with. The way we arrange the seats is, we change them every month, and every other time they get to choose where they want to sit. And on the times when they don't get to choose where they want to sit, they can still choose one person that they want to sit with. What it really comes down to is every other month they sit in a mixed gender group. Then when they get to choose where they want to sit—that will be April—they'll be back to all-boy groups and all-girl groups.
> *Carla:* Do they ever comment on that—do they notice?
> *Lucy:* Oh, we talk about it all the time. And I don't think it's bad, especially for the girls. I don't really like the idea of making them put up with all the shenanigans and nonsense that they would have to if they sat with boys all the time.

In this case Lucy thought it was fairer and more comfortable to support the division of girls and boys half of the time. She didn't like to require the girls to sit with the boys; she preferred to give them their choice. The seating groups chose their own names. The single-sex groups sometimes chose gender-specific names, for example, The Hula Hoop Girls and The X-Men, although there were also (very) neutral-sounding groups like The Blah Blahs.

I noticed that Lucy sometimes addressed her class as "girls and boys" or "boys and girls," and not surprisingly, so did her student teacher. I personally was taken aback by this, since it was one of the first things I gave up when I began thinking about sexism in connection with my teaching. Barrie Thorne calls this form of address the "verbal marking of gender" (1993, 34). Every time the teacher addresses her students in this way, she underscores the fact that the class is made up of two groups, females and males. This emphasis suggests that there is some relevance to the difference, though at the moment, if she is just calling them to the meeting circle, say, there may not be any relevance at all.

Lucy saw this matter differently, however. She said, "No, I say it a lot. I hate it when I fall into a pattern of saying "guys," you know, sort of generic *guys,* so I try to stop myself and say "boys and girls.""

Sometimes Lucy referred to a subgroup of the class by their gender. For instance, she pointed out that in doing a math worksheet "some of the girls" had elaborated the illustrations. She said, "you boys are being so rude" and summoned the "boys [who were] in the block area." Such "verbal marking" seems to emphasize division and difference rather than commonality.

The following scene, a discussion of a book written by two of the children, shows the children developing and questioning their own definitions of gender. As a background note, the previous year Lucy had read a set of her students' stories out loud and asked them to guess whether the author was a boy or a girl, which they were able to do in every case but one. She then suggested to them that they might try to write a different kind of story so that no one would be able to tell who wrote it.

Dolores and Rosie had written a book entitled "The Nightcrawler." What follows is the story as I later copied it from their draft. It had not yet been published and so was still written in invented spelling and invented punctuation. The beginning of each line indicates a new page. Dolores and Rosie ended each page with a period.

The Nightcrawler
   it was a Rainy night.
   the nightcrawler Was sleeping and.
   he woke up.
   he hraed a skreme. [heard a scream]
   He ran over.
   he ran all the way to the 4th floor but it was to lat the Killr.
   jumped out the window.
Chap. 2 got to find who that was
   He looked everywere but he cudent fined the killr and then he fined a
   werehouse and went in he saw Gun's and pistol's and.
he saw him he was smelling he was the human fly he.
   siad a fite to the finish. they fought and fought and fought. and the humen
   fly fataied [faded? fainted?] away. and
after that we never saw the humen fly agian.
                                        —by Dolores and Rosie

Dolores read the book to the class in the meeting circle in accordance to the class custom. She and Rosie sat together on the milk crate. It was usually Lucy's perch, but she turned it over to the authors on these occasions. After reading the story, the girls asked, "Any questions?" and then they called on different children.

This report of the book discussion comes from my field notes; it was not tape-recorded.

Karl:[4] It's different from the Barbie kinds of books you usually write.
Tom: Girls don't usually write about warehouses and guns and violence.
Reggie: [half to himself] Boys are violent.
Newman [or Karl?]: Girls in Robo-Cops are violent.
Noelle: It reminds me of Dog Story.
Reggie: Why do you always make books together?

Neil: [defending them] What's wrong with that?

Newman: Did you think of the idea together?

Karl: I like the title.

Harold: I like to see a change. I'd like to see boys writing different kinds of books.

Brianna: What made you think of it?

Rosie and Dolores: [responding in chorus, singsong, literally finishing each other's sentences] We worked on it a long time. We wanted to do something different. We wanted to make a book that had action in it.

Rosie: We thunk of the idea. [some discussion on the viability of *thunk*] This is the last question.

Ned: What are his powers?

Rosie and Dolores: He can jump rope [an interpolation of a "girls'" activity] to a third story window. He can make a sword come out of his hand.

Vic: I like the book. At first I thought it was copied, but it wasn't. I like the way you found a book you could agree on together.

Newman: Was it like phasing?

Rosie and Dolores: What's that? [Several boys chime in to explain a word they all seem to know. One suggests it's "like a ghost."]

Brianna: Will you write more?

Boy: Can he teleport?

Rosie: What is that? [Again, there are several attempts at explanation by the boys. Rosie thinks he can.] He goes through walls and comes back to life.

Larry: You just don't get it, Rosie.

Reggie: [trying to clarify] Like if he went into Mrs. Bennet's room, he'd just jump through that wall.

Lucy: Are you ready to have your book published?

Dolores: No, I have to check for periods.

The next story to be read aloud was "KILLR" by Neil.

Initially, in the fast-forward time of classroom interaction, Lucy and I both felt that this had been a positive discussion. The kids were engaged. There were many questions, some of which seemed to be encouraging. Lucy linked this discussion to the one that she mentioned from the previous year with many of the same children. She thought this was what Harold was alluding to when he said he'd like to see boys writing different kinds of books.

Lucy felt that the boys' comments were basically supportive, except for Larry's, "You just don't get it, Rosie." She did not agree with my interpretation, upon further consideration, that the conversation was subtly demeaning to the girls, that it revealed underlying assumptions about boy stories and girl stories, boy language and girl language, things boys know and things girls know.

In the first two responses, the boys express their surprise at the content of this story written by two girls. The girls say they "wanted to do something different" by writing "a book that had action in it," where action seems to imply violence. Neil, Newman, Karl, Harold, and Vic make comments that suggest qualified support, but then the boys begin to challenge the story and to compare the Nightcrawler with other characters they know about from television and movies. From the time Rosie says, "This is the last question," the boys move the discussion away from the book and begin to exclude the authors and put down the book with their superior knowledge of this genre. The boys use words like *phasing* and *teleporting* that are not used in the story and not even familiar to the authors. Harold's suggestion that boys might write "different kinds of books" is ignored.

The boys dominate this discussion. Rosie and Dolores are actively engaged in expanding on their book and answering questions, but for the most part, the girls in the audience act as bystanders. Brianna, who is from Bolivia, asks a question. Noelle, who is from Haiti, makes a connection. The White American girls are silent.

As I saw it, Dolores and Rosie had tried to break through gender stereotypes and make a literary foray into the boys' domain, but they lacked support and were beaten back. The outrageousness of their attempt is exemplified by the image of "jumping rope to a third story window," where Rosie and Dolores call upon a familiar girls' playground activity as a means to perform heroic feats.

In her book, *Gender Play*, Barrie Thorne writes about how schoolchildren sometimes play together in ways that assume boy/girl boundaries—games like "the girls chase the boys." She uses the term *borderwork* for interaction that cuts across—but is still based on—gender boundaries. She finds that such borderwork tends to emphasize gender as an "oppositional dualism" and to exaggerate rather than to bridge gender differences (1993, 86). In the discussion of "The Nightcrawler," the divisions remain and perhaps are even strengthened by the conversation.

Bronwyn Davies, an Australian researcher who also studies the construction of gendered identities, uses the phrase "category maintenance work" (1993, 18). In the children's discussion we can see these seven-year-olds not only acting in accordance with the culture's stereotypes but also forming their own and each other's ideas about the significance of gender. At the same time some of the children—Rosie, Dolores, and Harold in particular—are struggling individually *against* the dominant ideas.

A difficult challenge is illustrated by this episode: Two teachers (one the researcher) listened to this dialogue and initially saw it as positive—involved and focused. What would it take in such a case for teachers to be able to pick up more in real time? How could a teacher intervene in this discussion so that it would not demean or diminish either boys or girls, but would open up possibilities for all the children?

A second episode that involved most of the class in enacting gender divisions occurred on my second day in the classroom. When Lucy brought the children back from lunch, she was talking with Reggie and Tom about what they were going to do next. She had decided to give the class some free time. Letters, trading cards, and other things were suggested, but the two boys headed for the block corner.

Tom or *Reggie:* We're going to have a boys' side and a girls' side.
Lucy: You have to split the materials.
Tom: [to some girls who are in the block corner] You can have these.
Lucy: Wait. You don't get to decide who gets what.
Rosie: I don't want to have a girls' side and a boys' side.
Lucy: Tom, do you remember last time when we split the blocks? [Tom doesn't remember. I miss some here because just then Noelle came up with her letter and by the time I get back to the blocks, the decision to divide them has been made. After some tugging, the shelf that holds the blocks is moved to the middle of the area. There are different suggestions of how the division will happen, for example, a shelf for each group.]
Reggie: You can have this shelf and this. [Some discussion of who would have more space.]
Dolores: We can measure.
[Lucy gets out a yardstick. Meanwhile, Reggie and Tracy are splitting tiles. A compromise is worked out: both shelves are divided (unevenly) and marked by the kids, "BOYS" and "GRILS." The splitting goes on with great energy: Tracy, Reggie, Tom, and Ron are dividing the blocks, tiles, and various sticks. Noelle, Rosie, Dolores, and Brianna take some containers to the meeting circle and continue to divide things.]
Tom: This is working out real well. Too bad Rosie isn't here.
Lucy: She's in the meeting circle sorting things.
Tom: [with tiles] 1-2-3-4 for us! 1-2-3-4 for you!
[Reggie picks up Tom's refrain, and they chant together. Henry enters the block area. Tom greets him and hands him a container in which to split some small blocks.]
Reggie: Get off the girls' side, quick!
[Ron figures out that they can trade the large blocks, two halves for one whole. When they find odd numbers of things, the extras are called "out of the question" and put aside. Ron has found a clever way to wrap bundles of colored sticks. There is much talk of *ours* and *theirs*.]
Lucy: [to Rosie] Have you finished with the block project? If you are, I'd like you to finish your math.

Rita [a student teacher] flicks the lights for attention and suggests a sharing meeting. There are groans and loud comments. Lucy calls out a warning, "Boys in the block area!" The block sorting continues. There are squabbles over wall space and floor space. The girls put masking tape down the middle of the floor, leaving about one-third of the space for the boys and two-thirds of the space for the girls. In response to the complaints, Lucy suggests they both measure the perimeter [which is a current math vocabulary word]. Boys do foot lengths, girls do strides. They compare results. There is a lot of noise and squabbling. Lucy tells Ron to get off the girls' side.

Most of the children in the class were involved in this division of the block corner. Tom and Reggie were particularly excited about it, and their energy infected the other kids. Both girls and boys participated, in a together-yet-apart fashion that Thorne would call borderwork. There was a basic sense of equity as they counted out blocks and tiles, although other divisions were harder to equalize. The children showed considerable creativity, and they made some interesting math applications too. Rosie originally resisted, "I don't want to have a girls' side and a boys' side," but her objection, like Harold's in the previous scene, got swept aside. Later she joined in.

At the time Lucy appeared to sanction the boy/girl division. She called this activity "the block project" in speaking to Rosie, using a word that dignifies what they are doing and makes it an acceptable educational experience. She warned Ron off "the girls' side." Lucy went along with the children's division because she was curious about where it would lead, and she knew I would be interested too. After I had gone, she and the children discussed the effects of their experiment in the meeting circle.

A few days later in a phone conversation with Lucy, I learned that since that afternoon the block corner had been a source of constant friction. The boys were stealing the girls' blocks, and the kids were complaining. Soon afterward Lucy and Rita, the student teacher, rearranged the room and reintegrated the blocks.

Because of the kinds of problems that had been occurring with the blocks, Lucy decided to allow a single seating group to have the block corner for a whole week. This meant that only a small group would have access at any one time. During the months when Lucy assigned the seating groups, at least, girls and boys would be playing together. This small but significant change in practice resulted in a calmer block corner and served to encourage cross-gender interaction.

There were other times in the classroom when boys and girls were working or playing together easily. As Thorne (1993) points out, such moments tend to be ignored or downplayed by researchers who are usually looking for difference and contrast, but they are also important components of children's experience. In the following two scenes from my field notes, diverse groups formed spontaneously during free time. There seemed to be no gender conflict in these scenes, although the girls and boys did tend to play somewhat stereotypical roles:

The kids come in from recess. Roberta asks, "Can I play in the block corner?" Vic comes in, "Want to build something?" Leah joins them. They discuss roles. Vic will be the father, Roberta the mother, Leah—a child? Vic is building a police car out of pink Styrofoam blocks in one corner, Roberta is working on the house in the other. Roberta lays down some flat blocks for the basement. Vic says, "You don't know how to drive yet." They divide the long blocks one by one, discussing it quietly. Leah returns, starts taking blocks off shelves and splitting them. Roberta says, "I need a square one." Vic hands it to her.

During the same period of free time, a group of kids started a restaurant, The Taco Bell, where children of different races and sexes worked together amicably:

Brianna, Rosie, Ron, Tom, and Tracy are playing in the art corner, making food out of clay. Some of it looks quite realistic.

Brianna puts on an apron and takes orders on slips of paper from Lucy. Vic overhears the discussion of food. He says, "I'm going to be driving. I'm going to have dinner at a restaurant, then go to work." His police car is getting larger and larger, with blocks stacked in two sections. Roberta and Leah meanwhile have made a single block framework; the "floor" is in one corner. They lie down with round Styrofoam pieces for pillows.

Brianna comes over and takes my order for "food." Ron brings the food on a tray with pennies for change. Vic goes to the restaurant for his dinner. Rosie, using a pretend megaphone, asks for orders. "We're low on business," she says. They have a "car-through." Rosie, despairing of business from the outside, presses the button and puts in an order herself.

In subsequent years, when I visited Lucy's classroom, this kind of easy-going play in a diverse group was typical. It happened all the time. But that first year it was rare enough to be notable.

Gender and Race

Among the tensions in Lucy's classroom, gender often seemed to be a pre-eminent factor. Gender, compared with race, is more "speakable" in the classroom. In elementary schools, you frequently hear comments like, "Girls can't do that." "The boys won." "You boys stop that." Many classrooms still have separate lines for girls and boys. Teachers sometimes have spelling bees or math games in which the boys are pitted against the girls. Why do we tolerate these gender distinctions in schools today? We would not allow blatant distinctions based on race like: "White children can't do that." "It's the Black girls' turn." "Children of color line up here."

Among Lucy's students there was no open, stated opposition along lines of race, nothing like the boys' side and the girls' side of the block corner. When the children chose their own seating groups, not one of them was divided by race, whereas *all* of them were divided by gender. When I reexamined the "Responses during Reading Out Loud," which I presented earlier in the chapter, looking at race, I found that Lucy called on children of color and White children equally, whether they raised their hands or not. The children of color spoke out without raising their hands somewhat more, they were less apt to be silent, and the speaker "at length" was a child of color. The disparity was less than what I observed between the boys and the girls. As the children chose activities in their classroom, they seemed to hang with kids of other races and ethnicities quite comfortably. To me as an observer, the operations of race were not as obvious as those of gender in Lucy's classroom.

Nevertheless, in every classroom, race is a constant presence—in the bureaucracy of the school, in the teachers' relations with each other, in teachers' relations with kids and parents, in the curriculum, in kids' relations with each other, and in kids' perceptions of teachers. At least partly because of what Toni Morrison calls "the well bred instinct against noticing" (1992, 10), many White teachers do not see race clearly. Some even claim not to see race at all. I have many times heard teachers say, "Kids are kids. I treat them all the same." While this is manifestly untrue, these teachers must feel such statements show that they are not racist, rather than that they have not thought a lot about the subject. In her book *White Teacher* (1989), Vivian Paley, already a highly respected teacher and writer, tells of her own journey of self-discovery regarding issues of race. In Paley's case the initial impulse for her search came from issues that arose in her kindergarten classroom, children she felt she didn't understand or couldn't get through to. Similarly in my experience in Lucy's classroom, race called itself to my/our attention through areas of uncertainty and struggle.

Like most White Americans, when Lucy and I thought of issues of race, we thought of diversity and difference. We thought of "the other." We thought of children of color. We did not consider that we too are of a race. Unconsciously, we thought of ourselves as neutral, unraced. To that extent we fell into the widespread American habit of thought that assumes that the norm is White and the rest of the world is defined as other, if not lesser.

Writers like Toni Morrison, bell hooks, Lisa Delpit, Gloria Ladson-Billings, Sandra Harding, and others have exposed this habit of thought and have shown that there is no singular norm or standard and that White people are not at the center. We must shift our perspective, reposition ourselves and our angle of vision, in order to see ourselves as implicated in the issue of race, to see ourselves as others see us, to see how we still cling to the notion that we are at the center. The scenes in this section, how Lucy and I understood them at the time, and some thoughts I've had since then, might show how crucial this shifting of perspective is for teachers' understanding of all their students.

Lucy told me a story that shows race as a significant subtext in the kids' interactions. It also indicates how powerfully race and gender operate and *interlock,* to use bell hooks's verb (1989), even in second grade. Three children are involved in this story. Debbie, a White girl, has been mentioned before as the girl who was the most popular and the most silent in the classroom. In this story it's also significant that she had long, straight hair, which she wore loose. Noelle, one of the two Haitian children in the class, was a bright girl and very stylish. She wore her hair a different way almost every day. Karl was a big, tall, White boy who always wore outsized black T-shirts with designs and slogans of a rather destructive mode for a second grader. The first day I was there, his T-shirt said, "Here today, hell tomorrow."

This story came up when Lucy was telling me about Debbie's popularity. It worried Lucy that Debbie was so quiet and docile. It also bothered her that the children (especially the boys) would show such a preference for what appeared to be stereotypical female qualities. When the children chose their seating groups, everybody wanted to sit with Debbie.

> *Lucy:* That [the desk choosing] is one way I know that Debbie is the most popular girl in the class, and another way I know is, one recess I kept some boys who were horrible in the library after class to practice library behavior. At that particular time it was Karl, Larry, and Henry. And instead of just sitting there, we ended up having a long conversation. And they told me that they really liked Debbie.
>
> But another reason is, oh, this was so . . . Noelle. Noelle often goes running out of the room in tears. I don't mean often, but six times a year is often enough. And she went running out of the room hysterically in tears, loud crying. And I just let her go. When she came back, she sat in my lap, and I told her that I'd talk to her after school.
>
> After school she said, "Karl said something to me that was just so shocking, Ms. Dudley, it was so shocking! It was so shocking I don't know if I can tell you." I knew Karl could shock. Early in the year he had told Noelle to go suck his dick, and she hadn't really responded to that, so I thought, "Oh, no, but this can . . ." I wasn't sure I wanted to hear. I mean, there's a part of me that felt like, "Oh, no, I'll have to report it, and I don't even want to know. It's going to be something huge I'm going to have to deal with."
>
> Guess what he said to her? Finally I said, "Well, Noelle, tell me what it was." She said, "He told me that I should have hair like Debbie's!"

Distressing as it was, Lucy was glad Noelle had told her about Karl's remark, and she was glad Noelle had found it shocking. After school she talked to Noelle. She tried to explain to her that Karl had problems, and that's why he acted the way he did. Later she wished she'd drawn Noelle out more about her own feelings and reactions.

Lucy's telling of this story presents intricate issues about race, sex, language, and power—tough issues for anyone, let alone a second grader. These children are only seven years old, and already we can see in Karl's words the demeaning, objectifying, and sexualizing of the two girls. But it is objectification with a difference: The White girl is remote, silent, idealized; the Black girl is invidiously compared to her.

Another example of the complex operations of race and gender in the classroom was the daily interaction between Lucy and Reggie, the only African American boy in the class. Reggie was our first subject of conversation in the first interview. Lucy described him as "very dominant," and I noticed early on that he dominated my notes. Lucy felt that she had less authority in the class in Reggie's eyes, because she was White and because she was a woman. She believed that in Reggie's opinion, "As a White woman, I'm the lowest of the low." Nevertheless, she put enormous thought and energy into her relationship with this child. "He's a little gift to us, I think, because he brings such a different perspective and such struggle."

Reggie was one of the two children who came to school by bus from the city. At the end of the day, he and Rosie would have to hurry off to catch the bus for the long trip home, while the other children, who lived in the community, hung around waiting for parents or older siblings or for the after-school program to begin. This geographical distance, which also represented a cultural and economic difference, created a series of obstacles that would be challenging for any child.

Every morning Reggie would come in looking very neat with his shirt buttoned up to his throat. He would greet Lucy eagerly and politely, pick up his early morning work, and settle down. But during the course of the day, his behavior would deteriorate. I saw him hit other children several times, destroy other kids' work, jump over desks, and step on another child's ankle. He was by no means the only child in "the class from hell" who misbehaved or hurt others, but he was often at the center of any turmoil.

In trying to figure out Reggie, Lucy looked to his home and background as sources and explanations of his difficulties. These were more visible to her than the racism in the school or the cultural divide created by the busing program. Part of her interpretation of Reggie was that he suffered from "no bedtime stories." Her reference is to Shirley Brice Heath's book, *Ways with Words* (1983), which discusses how different groups of children are prepared by their families for school. Reggie's mother told Lucy that she had given away all his toys when he turned three, which shocked Lucy.

Lucy tended to see Reggie in terms of deficits, like "no bedtime stories." This, as Lisa Delpit (1995) points out, seems to be the interpretation many White teachers fall into because we have little knowledge of the experience of children of color, and indeed are unable to conceptualize their differences from ourselves as cultural. Gloria Ladson-Billings, making a similar point in her book *The Dreamkeepers*, speaks of the "stubborn refusal in American education to recognize African Americans as a distinct cultural group" (1994, 9). Thus educators do not inform ourselves of the characteristics of this culture or how we could make our educational system more "culturally relevant." Culturally relevant teaching is a central concept in Ladson-Billings's work, referring to teachers who, for instance, believe that all children can succeed, recognize students' own knowledge, reach out to their students beyond the classroom, connect with the wider community, and work to establish a community of learners.

Reggie was an only child, living with his mother who worked long hours. After school he was apparently home alone for long periods of time. Lucy said that on one occasion the principal kept trying to get in touch with his mother, calling her periodically during the day, but she did not return until 9 o'clock in the evening. At home Reggie did a lot of the housework, Lucy had learned. One day when I was there during recess, the coordinator of the busing program looked into Reggie's desk and said to me, "This is just too neat—look at this! That's not right for a kid his age." Reggie's orderliness and the responsibilities he took on at home were viewed as problems without acknowledging the strengths these implied. There were certainly children in that class who would not have been able to take care of themselves alone at home.

Lucy tried to understand what Reggie was going through in school. "Reggie feels lonely and outnumbered, because—what he really wants is to have a friend and to be liked and accepted, and he—because he doesn't play according to the same rules as the other kids, he can't figure it out yet. He can't—he hasn't figured it out, and I don't even know if he wants to play it their way. He may want—he may want them to accept him under his own terms."

In the last two sentences Lucy seems to question her own interpretation, as she wonders about Reggie's "own terms." In an earlier draft I wrote about Lucy seeing Reggie in "her terms," which she countered by saying that I described her in "my terms." Both of us were troubled by the challenge of seeing someone else in their own terms, and neither of us was able to see Reggie in *his* own terms.

Lucy's emphasis in discipline was on trying to get Reggie to see what he had done and to put it into words. One time Reggie got into a fight on the playground with Vic, Newman, and Tom, apparently hitting all three of them. The four boys were sent in, and Lucy spent an hour talking with them. On this occasion Lucy felt that her approach to the incident had worked. At the end of the hour's discussion, the children shook hands and decided that they would keep their desks together after all. As a result, Lucy said, "Reggie was just so happy. He was so relieved and so much lighter that these kids were still his friends. He did three times the amount of cleanup jobs that he's used to, because he just felt like, I mean he was on top of the world, because it had been settled without him being blamed."

Lucy was pleased with the results of this discussion, but she was concerned about the hour it took to get there and the fact that this took time away from the other kids. She is left with the problem, as she put it, "How do you make Reggie feel taken care of and the other kids feel taken care of too?"

One day when Lucy was out, the student teacher took over the class, and her supervisor, also a White woman, came in to observe. Lucy reported, "Rita's supervisor was really horrified at Reggie's behavior. She said he was just going around karate chopping kids indiscriminately. And how bad and inappropriate his behavior was. And when I hear that, I go nuts, because I know it's probably true, but, because I know I want to see progress so much and I do see it *in here*, then when I hear about how awful he is other places. . ."

For Lucy there was little institutional help available. There were no workshops, such as those Marcia teaches, to help White teachers understand the background and culture of other people's children and ways of discipline that they are used to. Lucy had tried on her own to get help in understanding and teaching Reggie. She discussed him with the African American teacher next door, who had suggested that Reggie needed more control. "I wouldn't let him get away with anything," she had said. His mother had told Lucy, "He's sneaky—better watch him!" Lucy thought the former advice glib and the latter unrealistic. How can you watch one child all the time in a classroom that has twenty-three children? On a day when the African American woman who worked in the busing program was there, watching him closely, I noticed that Reggie sat at his desk and worked hard, even after several other kids had finished their work and gone on to other activities.

Lucy's struggles with Reggie went on the whole year. Added to the other challenges raised by the "class from hell," Lucy finished the school year in a state of exhaustion instead of the exhilaration she usually gets from teaching. Reggie had a bad year too. What would have helped this situation? Like any teacher, Lucy had to deal with her students on the spur of the moment, with little time for reflection. What theory or advice unknown to her at the time or not yet available would have made a difference? What other questions should Lucy and I have asked? What would have helped us see Reggie in his own terms? Following are some suggestions, which I've presented in the form of general questions, because I think they are questions all teachers need to ask ourselves, even though I use Lucy's classroom as an example:

1. *What is the student's experience in the class? How was Reggie treated by the other kids?* Although I saw Reggie instigate a lot of trouble, he also tended to get blamed for things he hadn't done. One day when there was some fracas going on in the meeting circle, the kids blamed Reggie. Lucy pointed out that Reggie was on the opposite side of the room

at the time and could not possibly have done it. "Thank you!" said Reggie fervently.

Two New Zealand researchers, Adrienne Alton-Lee and Graham Nuthall (1993), studied a sixth grade classroom in a school that served a largely White, middle-class population. They used observers as well as videotapes, and in addition some of the children wore microphones that picked up a whole underworld of interactions that would not have been apparent to the teacher or an observer in the room. With these tools, the researchers analyzed a classroom incident and found the following sequence: First the teacher, a White man, in talking about the early settlement of New York City, referred to "White people," then "Europeans," then "us," identifying himself and most of the class with settlers in New York, but implicitly excluding Ricky, the only Maori child in the room. Then a student, Joe, turned to Ricky and under his breath called him, "Nigger, Samoan, Black man." Joe said Ricky was dumb and kicked him. Ricky kicked back. Ricky got reprimanded by the teacher. Later, the teacher was devastated to learn what had preceded this reprimand and how he had unconsciously aggravated the situation by his use of words. He would never have known about this whole sequence if it had not been for the elaborate technology being used in his classroom.

In Reggie's case, what unconscious racism did he pick up on, what teasing or meanness did he endure that Lucy or I could not see? There is always so much going on in a classroom. Some things the teacher will never know unless one of the children talks about it, as Lucy would not have known about Karl's hurtful remark, if Noelle had not confided in her.

2. *What happens in the hallways, at lunch, or at recess when aides are in charge?* Reggie was sometimes sent in as the cause of trouble. He had a school-wide reputation. How accurately were the aides able to see what was happening on a busy playground? Without strong communication between the aides and the teacher, for which there is not enough time, this disconnect between experiences in the classroom and on the playground can create or exacerbate problems for students.

3. *How does the student see the teacher?* To Reggie was Lucy his familiar, warm, supportive Ms. Dudley, or was she merely White Teacher? It is crucial for teachers not only to see our students from different perspectives but to turn our analysis on ourselves, to see ourselves, as Lisa Delpit puts it, "in the unflattering light of another's angry gaze" (1995, 46).

4. *What cultural information does the teacher need to know in order to teach this particular student?* Delpit stresses the importance of knowing the

cultural background of "other people's children," meaning poor children as well as children of color, if we are to teach them successfully. Unfortunately, this background is not usually part of our training as teachers. Not only that, most of us in our years in school have learned a social studies taught from a single perspective, that of White male victors, and full of stereotypes that make us, if not despise, at least dismiss the perspectives of others. To counteract these stereotypes and to broaden our perspectives we need new, immediate, essential information that can perhaps best come from the community itself. "No individual can be expected to understand the intricacies of every culture without the assistance of members of those cultures" (Delpit 1995, 123). Lucy did ask the African American teacher next door and Reggie's mother for help, but their advice did not seem helpful to her. At the time she could not use it as a way to take another look at her own practice.

5. *What do teachers need to perceive about themselves and their own practice?*
   Lisa Delpit would say that Lucy could not hear the advice she had herself sought. As Delpit points out in "The Silenced Dialogue," it is often the hearing—the *really* hearing—that is the greatest challenge between cultures. Our own notions of teaching, students, manners, authority, and learning interfere with our perceptions and prevent us from seeing—from *really* seeing—the student who stands in front of us. "We do not really see through our eyes or hear through our ears but through our beliefs. To put our beliefs on hold is to cease to exist as ourselves for a moment—and that is not easy" (1988, 297).

   Really hearing and seeing and "ceasing to exist as ourselves for a moment" imply a dramatic, disruptive, and probably painful encounter with ourselves. What are we assuming? What are we not seeing? Should we change our practice?

   As an example of cultural difference, in discussing teaching strategies that seem to work with African American children, Delpit mentions using explicit language and "displaying a high degree of personal power" (1995, 168). Was Reggie looking for a more tangible form of power? Is this why Lucy felt he considered her as a White woman, the "lowest of the low?" Perhaps he was expecting that a teacher would display more personal power, and it was not happening in Lucy's classroom. Perhaps the long discussions of his behavior only baffled him. Can teachers change our practice to reach all our children? Should Lucy change her preferred way of doing things in the classroom for one child?

In one of the last of our many talks about Reggie, I asked Lucy what she thought would make a viable school situation for him. Her response was hesitant, but she said that she felt he would be better off in a school where the teachers were African American and at least half of the kids were too—a recognition, I felt, that some of his issues were cultural. Later, when I was in Marcia's classroom, I thought of Lucy's response many times. I could imagine that Reggie would feel comfortable in Marcia's class.

But this is no solution. White teachers must strive for ways to make kids like Reggie comfortable and successful now in our own classes. This is a widespread challenge today, when the numbers of teachers of color are decreasing in proportion to White teachers, while the proportion of children of color is increasing in schools throughout the country (Ladson-Billings, x).

Furthermore, race alone is not the entire issue here; there are broader issues of culture as well. Delpit mentions that African American teachers from a middle-class background "who do not identify with poor African American students they teach may hold similar damaging stereotypes" and can have problems very similar to middle-class White teachers (1995, xiv). Ladson-Billings's book describes the practice of both African American and White teachers who were the "dreamkeepers," or successful teachers of African American children.

Not really seeing, not really hearing, not taking the other seriously, not being able to see another's point of view, not being able to acknowledge our own privilege, not being able to turn the light of questioning on ourselves. Does this sound familiar? Yes, we've been there—when the same issues, which were so palpable and crucial and obvious to women, were not apparent to most men. They felt they could ignore them. Over time some men saw the light, some began to change their ways, some never have been able to get what we are talking about. Women who have experienced such powerlessness and frustration cannot want to perpetrate it again. We cannot ignore vital information about others, and, just as important, about ourselves.

This is a difficult though crucial task. As Peggy McIntosh points out in an article on White privilege (1989), if we are not conscious of these prejudices and actively fighting against the perpetration of such ideas in our institutions, in our relations with others, and in our own souls, then we are teaching these same ideas—unconsciously, perhaps, but transmitting them nonetheless. In this way we are ensuring that another generation will maintain the same prejudices and blind spots and oppression in its many forms.

Power, Teaching, and Mothering

The issue of how the teacher asserts her power in the classroom has long been a loaded one for White, middle-class women, who are not expected to be familiar with power or to be acknowledged as persons with power, but are nevertheless required to exercise power in order to keep their classes in order. This was a concern of the early schoolmen and of superintendents in the mid-1900s as they watched women enter teaching in greater and greater numbers. Would they be able to control the class? The drama of a teacher having to assert herself over an unruly class, sometimes against her desire to be a loving and loved teacher, has been a compelling subject of fiction. Ursula Brangwen in D. H. Lawrence's *The Rainbow* suffers when the situation in the classroom requires her to thrash a student. Lucy Snowe in Charlotte Bronte's *Villette* relishes her triumph after she has finally gained control of the class by locking an obstreperous young woman in a closet. Power, as in Lucy's struggles with Reggie, can make us feel uncomfortable and ambivalent.

In a society where men are more frequently in positions of authority and more apt to be seen as invested with authority, it is harder for women to gain the respect of the class. Lucy observed, "There are sometimes students who think that they don't need to listen to me because I'm a woman." I used to feel somewhat envious of what appeared to me to be such easy control on the part of a male colleague. For one thing, I envied his voice, which, though gentle, could always be heard *under* the voices of his students and commanded swift attention, while women's voices tend to be in a range similar to children's. And of course we don't want to be shrill. So much of authority is conveyed through the voice.

The issue of power in the classroom comes up especially frequently for a teacher who deals with a difficult class. Lucy questioned when to use it and when not to. In talking about an interview for her first classroom teaching job, she used the word *controlling* to express her sense of a negative use of power.

> *Lucy:* I was very fortunate to be hired by a principal who wanted me to promote my style in a public school. I wasn't sure that I wanted the job, so I approached the interview as radically as I felt comfortable doing, and I thought, If I represent myself 100 percent the way I really feel and still get hired, well, then that's OK.
>
> At the time it was risky, because I did need a job, but it worked out very well. She really liked what I had to say, and she wanted me to help other teachers to loosen up and become less *controlling* and—noisier. [laughter]

Lucy felt confident in her own abilities when she first taught full time. Similarly when she started to teach in her present position, she felt "practically cocky with confidence and said exactly what I thought all of the time." She sees herself as the "ultimate power" in the classroom, but she does not like to use this power with a heavy hand. The following passage from an interview reveals Lucy's reasons for preferring a light touch and connects this with the theme of her desire to understand her students and her concern about the feelings, understandings, and attitudes that underlie their behavior. It also repeats her sense of *control* as a negative aspect of power:

> *Carla:* Um, do you think that your ideas—your style of teaching—do you see your style of teaching as related to your feminist ideas?
> *Lucy:* Mm-hmm.
> *Carla:* How so? [mutual laughter at the failure of my yes/no question]
> *Lucy:* Maybe not. I think that can surface more easily because I'm less controlling, and if they can surface then they can be worked on.
> *Carla:* What do you mean "they can surface?"
> *Lucy:* Issues—the issues that come up. So if I'm keeping the children quiet when I read a story to them, how would I know who's more dominant and who needs to speak out more, for example? If I made them sit in rows. . . I think the more control you have, the less you have an opportunity to work on any kind of issue.

This quote shows Lucy's sense of the double-edged quality of power and her recognition that her approach to discipline, like any approach, has its problematic side. Among the issues and feelings that can surface when control is loosened are gender differences and antipathies, and once these are brought to the surface, the teacher is in the position of having to decide what to do about them. If she does not keep tight control of the discussion, how can the girls—who are less loud and aggressive—have their fair share of airtime?

> *Lucy:* When you're sitting there you think, those kids don't wait a minute to say what they really think or feel—to say what they *feel*. But they don't want to say what they *think*. [laughter] And I am just very conscious of making sure the girls get their turn, but they need me to do that. I don't want to encourage them to yell more or be more aggressive, but I'm also not particularly effective. I wouldn't say ineffective, but I am not [sigh], I don't want to have the kind of classroom control where everybody has to be quiet and wait till they're acknowledged, so I don't repress the boys.

Research shows that more tightly controlled discussions—at least discussions led by a teacher conscious of the issues and striving for equity—tend to be more gender-equitable (Krupnick 1993; Sadker and Sadker 1994). This is a dilemma for teachers who want their classrooms to be equitable and also want them to be relatively free, lively environments. Lucy's "class from hell" brought these matters to a head. In other years her approach worked more smoothly. The previous year, for instance, she didn't have to ask kids to raise their hands at all in circle meetings.

I witnessed what I considered a brilliant use of teacher power one day when Lucy, with a few deft strokes, completely changed the tenor of a discussion.

The math circle assembles very quickly. The kids are asking, "Can we work with a partner?" before Lucy even starts. "Yes," she says, then changes her mind: "No, I want you to work in your groups, because I want you to get to know the kids in your group." There are voices calling out, saying, "But we already know them." Lucy says, "Brianna has her hand up." Brianna asks, "What if they don't like you?" There are other similar negative reactions.

Lucy asks, "Do you remember how last time when we had new groups you made new friends? Who can remember a new friend—someone they didn't always like?" She gives an example of how Reggie and Henry didn't use to be friends. Then lots of hands go up and kids name their new friends: Roberta mentions Leah; Noelle names Rosie; Rosie names Nora; Reggie mentions Henry; Karl names Reggie and Henry, Brianna mentions the inseparable Debbie and Raina; and so on. Although girls only mention girls and boys, boys, many of the pairs are interracial, and everyone in the class gets named at least once. It's a complete turnaround and a lovely moment. It seems so reaffirming to have someone say out loud you're their friend. Lucy says, "Good job, class. I'm really proud of you for working together so well." She explains the assignment: to write as many fractions as they can think of that are less than one. They divide up from the meeting and go off to work with their new friends.

In this discussion Lucy changed the spirit of the class in such a way that the children not only said positive things to each other, at the end of the discussion they also were ready to act in a more cooperative manner.

In the classroom, anger can be seen as an aspect of control gone somewhat awry. I saw all three of the case-study teachers get angry momentarily at individual students or the whole class. On my first afternoon in Lucy's class, she got angry at Rosie. Lucy does not apologize for her reaction:

> *Lucy:* I mean, I'm not ashamed of what I do. You probably could tell that. I'm a little more self-conscious in that—in the best of all possible worlds I wouldn't have to take Rosie's book away from her, and as soon as I take it away, I know, "Oh, I shouldn't have done that; now she's crying." But also, I know that you know too. This is a teaching day. These things happen. Moment to moment you do the best you can, and nine times out of ten you're hitting the nail on the head all right.

On another occasion she talked about a conversation she had with Rita, the student teacher, and her supervisor about a stormy class meeting that Rita had struggled to control:

> *Lucy:* Well, I stood up for Rita, because I said, "You know, the trouble with this group—even when I stepped in, I had trepidations," because I feel a little bit like—with you here [meaning the researcher] and with her supervisor here—I feel a little bit, when you get strict with children, it's very controversial, and I feel there's a big part of me that says, "They're going to think I'm a bad person for doing this. They're going to think nobody should talk to kids this way, but I can't stand another minute. I'm going to do it anyway."

There's a part of me that feels that way. And that's the part of me that I was trying to describe to you that I call my mother part, because it's almost as if I'm the mother of all these kids—and damn, I would never let one of my kids act that way. I would *never* let my kid be so out of control and so disrespectful. If Lesley or Hal acted that way, I would speak to them in a second. So that's kind of how I feel. I can't stand it another minute. It's rude, and it's disrespectful, and that's the bottom line.

Anger and "getting yelled at" were important themes in Lucy's story of her own schooling and can be seen to connect with feelings she has as a teacher. Although she does not apologize for her anger, she feels that she might be seen as "a bad person" if she gets angry at the kids. She is faced with a difficult quandary. The middle-class values she was brought up with, of fairness, of politeness, of not showing your anger, conflict with the need to express her own feelings and to control a difficult class.

> *Lucy:* Um, I think ultimately, especially in this group of children, I do let them know that I have the power. As you can tell, I have given up some of my middle-class views like, "You need to sit down now" [polite voice]. I'm much more apt to say, "Rosie, sit down" [peremptory tone].

This contrast Lucy draws between politeness and directness will be echoed by Marcia in chapter 4. In the workshops Marcia taught for teachers working in inner city schools, the participants, who were mostly White, thought the language of some teachers of color "too strong." Marcia urged them to use a clearer, more direct style in addressing their students, rather than the indirect, overly polite style often associated with teachers. Lucy was aware of this issue.

Lucy did not rely on elaborate rules as a source of authority. A fellow teacher, by contrast, had posted on his walls no fewer than forty-two separate rules, mostly kid-generated. Lucy did not want to spend time settling arguments over so many rules. She said that she relied basically on the Golden Rule.

> *Lucy:* I usually. . . you can hear me—"I really don't want you kids to get up before I've dismissed you. You just get up and start walking back to your desks. I haven't finished telling you what I need to tell you." I said that today. I mean, I don't have a written-down rule that says, "Children will stay in the meeting circle until the teacher tells them to leave." They're just supposed to guess that. And I have the ultimate power.

Lucy sounds ironic when she says, "They're just supposed to guess that." She realizes the gap in her own logic. In such a diverse class the Golden Rule, "Do unto others as you would be done by," may not be a very clear or reliable guide to behavior, particularly since there is considerable variation in how children think they "would be done by."

Another power issue that ran like a theme through our conversations was the contentious connection between teaching and mothering. This association has deep historical roots, going back to the nineteenth century. At that time (and well into the twentieth century in many places), mothers could not be teachers. They had to give up their teaching positions when they married. Nevertheless, in the move to increase the numbers of women teachers, Catharine Beecher and other educational leaders sought to reframe teaching as a good preparation for motherhood (Sklar 1973).

All three of the case-study teachers mentioned connections they saw between mothering and teaching. Of the three, however, Lucy was the only one who was herself a parent,[6] and she thought that had been important for her as a teacher. She felt that she had learned from her son and daughter a lot that was useful to her in her teaching. In the passage quoted previously, Lucy associates mothering and teaching, "And that's the part of me that I was trying to describe to you that I call my mother part, because it's almost as if I'm the mother of all these kids—and damn, I would never let one of my kids act that way."

As with mothering, the demands of teaching sometimes seem endless, and it is often hard to set boundaries. In describing the fruitless efforts she had made to help the music teacher deal with his class, Lucy finally said, "I'm sick of it. I can't help everybody." During one interview, after a day of extreme ups and downs, Lucy was particularly tired and discouraged, and here was Ron coming in more than an hour after school, very upset because he couldn't find his sweatshirt. That was the afternoon when Lucy said, "After a day like this, I don't feel I'm doing anything that different."

I was in Lucy's classroom just before Mother's Day, one of the numerous holidays that require elaborate preparation in elementary school classrooms. It was also a day that was freighted for both Lucy and me. We had talked together about our elderly mothers, who lived at a distance from us, our children, and our changing relationships with both generations.

There had been a lot of interest in trading cards that year, and Lucy, basing her curriculum as she frequently did on the children's interests, decided to have the class make trading cards for their mothers. Instead of a superhero, they would draw their mother on one side of the card and on the other side give her a rating for each of several characteristics. The cards would then be laminated so that they would look spiffy—like real trading cards. The kids loved the idea. As a group they discussed what characteristics would be appropriate. They decided to use some of the ones usually found on trading cards, such as Strength, Speed, Intelligence, Stamina, and to add Love. They discussed each quality and how it could relate to their mothers and what their mothers do—like making breakfast, going to work, comforting them when they have bad dreams. It turned out that the children didn't really know what Stamina meant, and they wondered if this characteristic would be appropriate for their mothers? Lucy looked it up in the dictionary. She read the definition aloud to them: "the ability to endure fatigue." Lucy and I both cracked up at what seemed to us a definition of "women's work." Yes, we thought, this could be an appropriate characteristic to use on their Mother's Day trading cards. The word *stamina* came up frequently in our conversations thereafter.

Teaching had a strong history among the women of Lucy's family, with her three teacher-aunts. Lucy felt "annoyed" by the fact that teaching is such a female occupation:

> *Lucy:* Well, it's a female-dominated occupation, and that's annoying to me sometimes. . . . I know that if men apply for a job at my grade level, they're given priority because there aren't very many of them, which is amusing to me, because I certainly know that the reverse isn't true. For example, if a woman wants to be an engineer, she has to work much *harder* to be an engineer. She's not—people aren't dying to have women as engineers. But I know, for example, the third grade teacher, who's new this year, was hired because he's a man. He actually said to another teacher he would help balance out the teaching staff in the primary grades, and by that was meant, it would have a better male representation. I don't like that.
>
> *Carla:* Do you think there's anything to that argument?
>
> *Lucy:* No. I actually—I don't know what to think about that, Carla. I think women are not—are—whether they're natural nurturers or not, as it is right now in time, we do a lot more nurturing, and we're asked to do endless nurturing, and that annoys me.

The things that annoy Lucy about teaching seem to be the things that annoy her about the position of women in this society generally, and teaching sometimes seems to Lucy to maintain rather than to transform this position. She does not see women's nurturing as necessarily "natural." She questions that essentialist position. She says, "As it is right now in time," women do the nurturing. Elsewhere she speculates that the reason women are the nurturers in this society is that this is something men don't want to do, which is a reference to a view of a patriarchal society in which men define roles for women.

Besides the "annoying" aspects of teaching, the aspects associated with the traditional female role, there is another side of teaching that Lucy finds far more appealing.

> *Carla:* So what do you think of teaching as a job for a feminist, then?
>
> *Lucy:* Teaching appeals to me not because I'm a feminist, but it appeals to me because it's so variable and unpredictable. And because I can use my intuition more than I could in a lot of other occupations.

The characteristics of teaching that Lucy mentions here—variable, unpredictable, intuitive—recall her long-term interest in art, the creative and expressive quality of her teaching, and her desire to help her students discover and express their own ideas and feelings. These characteristics seem to indicate a way out of the oppressive, overly responsible, motherly aspects of teaching. They remind us that teaching, in addition to its annoying qualities, has abundant opportunities for liberation.

Although in her statement Lucy is making a distinction between teaching and feminism, the descriptive words she uses strike me as eminently feminist. In fact they remind me of the end of Denise Riley's book *Am I That Name?: Feminism and the Category of 'Women' in History*. In this book Riley recounts the many different ways *Woman* has been defined over the centuries (most frequently by those other than women). She finds that the variation is so great that she can hardly identify a single quality that has been insisted on consistently. In the face of this, what can we say about feminism? What qualities does feminism require? Riley concludes, rather like Lucy, that we need "to develop a speed, foxiness, versatility" (1990, 114) that will enable us to act, to fight for the rights of all women, and to explore the further possibilities of feminism.

NOTES

1. See the Life History Interview in appendix B.

2. Here and elsewhere I use a question mark to indicate the way Lucy ended some of her statements with a questioning tone.

3. The significance of this particular word will be explained in the last section of this chapter.

4. The race and ethnicity of the children who speak in this discussion: Dolores and Rosie, the authors, are Haitian and African American, respectively; Brianna is Bolivian; Noelle is Haitian; Reggie is African American; Karl, Tom, Newman, Neil, Harold, Ned, and Larry are White; Vic is from India.

5. This combination of kids resulted from the new policy; these three were in the same seating group.

6. Although this was true at the time, since then Rosemary has become the legal guardian for her two young nieces.

3

Rosemary:
Finding a Political Voice

What would happen if one woman told the truth about her life? The world could split open.

—Muriel Rukeyser

What difference does it make?

—Robin

As I was finishing up my observations in Lucy's classroom, I heard about a fifth grade teacher in a nearby town who was a feminist and a lesbian—and was known by her students and their parents to be a lesbian. I was amazed. At that time, the fall of 1993, I had never known or even heard of a lesbian elementary school teacher who was "out" to her class in a public school. I had supposed that it would be hard to locate a teacher who was lesbian—and very tricky to talk and write about her experiences in a way that would not endanger her teaching life. From my own experiences with friends and fellow teachers and from what I had read, I imagined a lesbian teacher would have to be carefully closeted. The work of Madika Didi Khayatt (1992), for example, who interviewed eighteen lesbian teachers in Ontario, details how painstakingly and at what personal cost the teachers hid their lesbian identities. In her book *The Last Closet* (1996), Rita Kissen interviewed more than a hundred gay, lesbian, and bisexual educators across the United States. She found that all of them wanted to be out in their schools, although few had found the combination of circumstances that would allow them to come out. Most of these teachers were still closeted at work and forced to live with painful feelings of alienation from their true selves and with the constant fear of exposure.

Not so Rosemary. When I first called her and said that I was looking for feminist elementary school teachers, she said unhesitatingly, "Well, I qualify!" I was glad she was so direct. I mentioned how some of the teachers I had called were rather hesitant to call themselves feminists. "It's because they think it means lesbian," she said. "That's why they deny the label. I'm a lesbian myself."

Rosemary's forthrightness is an important part of who she is. It is the result of certain decisions she has made about her life. She is committed to being out, to talking about what that means, and to making her perspective known. Her perspective gives her Sandra Hardings's "epistemological advantage," that vantage point where she can see what others might miss, as she talks about her life and her work in the following pages. My perspective, on the other hand, is subject to distortion from heterosexual privilege and its consequent blind spots.

People who are heterosexual are often not aware of how fundamentally heterosexist this society is in its assumptions, and how its institutions, such as schools, are likewise. Because of these assumptions, heterosexuals have certain inherent privileges, of which they are often unaware. One unfortunate aspect of being in a position of relative privilege—being male or White or heterosexual or able-bodied, for example—is that we are often unaware of the privilege conferred by these qualities. We think of them as merely the norm, not as aspects of privilege. In the first chapter I mentioned Peggy McIntosh's (1989) metaphor of an "invisible knapsack" of privilege that White people carry. Here is the same kind of phenomenon—the invisible privilege that attaches to being heterosexual in this society.

An exchange that occurred early on in Rosemary's classroom helped make this privilege visible. In the middle of a class discussion, Heather, one of Rosemary's students, said, "There's a rumor that Mr. Morse is gay. Everyone is saying that."

Rosemary's response was, "Does that make a difference? Does that affect how good he is as a teacher?"

Another student, named Robin, chimed in, "It's nobody's business. What difference does it make?"

This interesting conversation was cut off by the bell for the bus students, but later Rosemary and I came back to it. I said, "I interpreted Robin as meaning—because your first response was, 'Does it matter? Does it make any difference in terms of his teaching ability?' I thought Robin was following up on that."

Rosemary responded, "I don't know. Well, when I hear that—when people say, 'It doesn't matter—it's their personal life,' to me it says, 'It *does* matter,' because everyone else's personal life—everyone else talks about their family, you know. Everyone's life here is public. Nancy [an aide in her room] talks to you about her kids and her family all the time."

I felt a pang. It had not occurred to me to think of chatting about my family as a privilege, though it was very clear to Rosemary and would be to anyone who has felt they had to resort to "the Monday morning pronoun"[1] in talking about what they did over the weekend.

That privilege was invisible to me, and so was my own guardedness. At the time I hardly noticed how very selective I was in mentioning that two of my daughters are lesbians. One lesbian daughter is almost acceptable these days, but two takes some absorbing. I had, of course, told Rosemary, but I had not told Nancy.

In this second case study I began to see that the ground on which I had placed a bunch of assumptions was giving way. Some things I shared with Lucy—feminism, teaching, Whiteness, middle-classness—I also shared with Rosemary, but the difference in sexuality made a difference in the way we looked at and operated in the world.

I have mentioned how different the three case-study teachers were and how the differences influenced what I learned in each classroom. An interactive, participatory mode of research implies that different situations and individuals will require different approaches and responses. I was not always sure of my path. As a teacher I had certainly been aware of how much both teacher and learner can get out of what might be labeled a "mistake." As a researcher, it took me a while to relearn this lesson. I found that misinterpretations, misunderstandings, contradictions, and moments when I crossed the researcher line could yield material and insights I might otherwise have missed. I became more interested in the play of differences among the three classrooms and in what my experiences there might reveal.

ROSEMARY'S STORY

The issues that Rosemary and I talked about—feminism, education, activism, lesbianism—were things she loved to talk about, and she welcomed the opportunity my research provided. "When else do I get a chance to talk about these things?" she asked. She recalled how, when she was growing up, the members of her extended family loved to talk, especially about politics. "Every Friday night my grandparents and uncle would come over, and all we would talk about was politics." They were "news junkies," who devoured newspapers and later news programs on TV.

Her family lived in a small town in Connecticut, where she was born. Her father was a lineman for the local electric company. Her mother stayed home and raised their four children. There was never much money, and they lived in housing projects.

Rosemary connects her family's strong feelings about politics with their own position in life. She said, "Well, I think they're, they were avid Roosevelt Democrats, *you know*, Franklin Roosevelt, and they were people that, they saw the Democratic Party, and, *you know*, politics is a way to get a fair shake, and they clearly weren't getting a fair shake in their lives, *you know*. They were bright people who should have gone to college and for— but—*you know*, it wasn't available, so I think they looked to politics as a way to, *you know*, create fairness.

Sometimes Rosemary's speech is hesitant as she wrestles with a question. When I showed her a draft of the case study, she said that the thing that surprised her the most was how hesitant she sometimes sounds (on paper) when talking about her work. The passage above is sprinkled with the phrase *you know*. This phrase, as well as the earnestness of her tone, suggests to me a desire to make me understand and also a sense of the risk that she is taking in telling me about her life. Rosemary's interpretation, when she read a draft of this chapter, was that *you know* indicated a feeling of "kindred spirits." At other times, her voice gathers momentum when she hits on a favorite story or a point she feels very strongly about. Then she speaks eagerly, her ideas getting ahead of her and tumbling out in long sentences.

In the previous quotation, Rosemary presents her parents as limited by their circumstances and their class position, rather than by their own abilities. Her interpretation of events in this life story tends to emphasize such political and structural influences, in addition to personal and psychological ones.

As Rosemary saw it, her father's opportunities were constrained early on by a decision he made, which Rosemary considered to be an ethical and responsible one: He had a chance to go to college, as his father and grandfather had done, but he turned it down because he was the sole support of his mother. Then during World War II he wanted to leave his job with the electric company for more lucrative employment in the war industry, but his work was considered essential to the war effort, and he was not allowed to leave. Later he started a union at his place of work, and that activity also hindered his chances for advancement.

Rosemary's mother had worked for Aetna Insurance before she was married. Her leaving this position makes a poignant tale. As Rosemary told it, "The best years of her life were before she got married. She got married when she was twenty-nine. She worked in Hartford. Now it's about a half-hour drive at sixty miles an hour, but then it was a big deal. And so her friends—you know Hartford's the capital, so people came in from all over the state to work there—so her friends were from all over. When she got married, she never saw them again."

She was fired from her job when she got married, which was the practice of the insurance company at that time (the thirties)—as well as of many other employers, such as schools. She and her husband moved to a housing project "which wasn't near anything." There was no public transportation, and she was trapped. Rosemary's interpretation was that, "Through her marriage she had lost all her self-confidence." Here she tells how her understanding of her mother's life has changed, how her interpretation of the structural and societal forces limiting her mother's life has mitigated the sense of blame she felt growing up (here again I have italicized certain words):

> *Rosemary: I think* I was highly motivated by my mother's life. *I mean*, I just saw her life as such a tragedy, *you know,* a bright, capable woman, who, because of classism and sexism, was limited—and also marriage and the power dynamics of marriage and also, *I think,* my parents' personalities. *I mean,* my father always had to be right—and that's a hard thing to work with, if he always gets to be right—because you're a woman.
> *Carla:* Yes, you're always allowed to be right—
> *Rosemary:*—because you bring home the bacon. *I mean,* I even told my mother that. I said, "You know, I'm a feminist." It certainly was a reaction to her life—things had to be better for women. And, *I think,* once—I used to always blame her—*I mean,* my father would come home from work, and she'd be complaining, unhappy, and, *you know,* I saw my mother as always nagging, always after Dad, and *I think,* when I got older and understood what her life was like, I used to talk to her about that, *you know,* and that she shouldn't feel that there was something wrong with her—that she did something wrong—it was like, *you know,* there's the personal aspect, but there's the institutional.

In this passage, as Rosemary tries to figure out and explain the meaning her mother's life holds for her, she uses repeated phrases—*I think, I mean,* and the aforementioned *you know*—that convey a sense of struggle and risk as well as shared understanding. She sees her mother as having abilities she never got to use or develop because of her position as a working-class wife and mother at a particular time in history. Rosemary feels very strongly about this, calling it "a tragedy."

Although most of Rosemary's education was in Catholic schools, she went to kindergarten at a public school, because it was closer to home. Her mother didn't want her to walk as far as the Catholic school, although Rosemary recalls her older brother had. She remembers liking the crafts and different projects in kindergarten. After that year she transferred to the Catholic school, where she was taught by nuns. She thinks the nuns, for the most part, probably didn't have any choice about teaching, and she wonders how much training they had and how happy they were in their work. Again, looking back, she doesn't blame them, but sees the limitations placed on them.

When I asked Rosemary how she remembered herself as a student, she recalled a teacher she both feared and liked. She is still rather puzzled by this remembered ambivalence. In this passage, the words that refer to her fear are italicized.

> *Rosemary:* Uh, I liked school if I liked the teacher, I think, you know. I mean I remember liking certain teachers. I remember liking my friends, and I only remember—like if I was *afraid*—like I had a fifth grade teacher who was very—I think very *strict*. I don't know if she was *mean*, but she was very, very *strict* and I used to be *afraid*—like I would be *afraid* not to do my homework. And I also remember that when I left that class, to move on to the next year, I cried. So looking back, I think, well, I must have liked her, but she *scared* me. It was weird. There must have been part of her that obviously was a positive, but I remember, like being *afraid* of her.
>
> *Carla:* And even as you remember you can't make sense of it, if you were afraid?
>
> *Rosemary:* Yeah, so I think, I must have liked this person. You know, it's funny.

Here Rosemary speaks in a hesitant manner, interrupting herself as she tries to piece together this contradictory memory. Lucy had also recalled her fears about school. It is disturbing to find that for both women their most vivid memories of school evoke fear.

In general Rosemary remembers her education as dry and unvarying. "We sat in our seats all day, and we worked from workbooks and textbooks." She found different things to interest her from time to time. She enjoyed politics, science, and math, but for the most part she found her schooling boring. At the time she wondered why anyone would want to teach.

Rosemary had one older and two younger brothers. The distinction between the boys and the one girl in the family was underscored by the distribution of household chores. The boys did the outside jobs and had access to their father's power tools. Rosemary envied the boys their jobs, especially the use of the tools, which she was denied. Years later, as an adult, she made up for this. She took a woodworking course and used power tools with her kids in the classroom. As a child, however, her lot in life was to do the ironing. She ironed shirts for all three of her brothers.

I asked Rosemary whether, in addition to these stereotypical chores, she had any childhood memories of times when she was aware that it made a difference that she was a girl and not a boy. Like Lucy, Rosemary's memory involves "getting yelled at." In both of their stories yelling is used to enforce compliance with the traditional female role, and for both women, it became part of a vivid memory:

Rosemary: Well, I remember we lived near a woods, and we all used to go into the woods and climb trees, and I always had to climb—like I had to prove—I felt I had to be better than the boys—like climb the highest, you know. I mean, that was really important to me. And my older brother, I had to do whatever he did and more.

Carla: Well, it's still true for women. [laughter]

Rosemary: Yeah. Right. I remember I was dressed up for church on Easter Sunday, or whatever. I remember climbing this tree, and I had church shoes on. I don't know whether they were patent leather, but they were slippery, not things to climb with, and I got really high and scared myself. I should never have done that, and I got yelled at, but you know that was important to me that I was as good as they were, that way.

She was competitive with her older brother and wanted to be able to do what he did. The two of them played hooky together on occasion. They also shared a newspaper route. Of course, as she told me, the route was officially his, because at that time girls could not have paper routes, but the two of them shared the work and the income equally. It seems wonderfully ironic in light of her long-standing interest in the news and her later work for women's rights that Rosemary was a "newsgirl" before this was even an allowable occupation for a girl.

In high school in the late 1950s, she and her older brother were both very interested in the news and politics. A social studies teacher let her read *Advise and Consent* and *The Congressional Record* in class while the other students followed the regular curriculum. Rosemary doesn't remember that any of her friends shared her interest in politics—just her brother. His interest and ability helped him go on to prep school, college, and law school. Rosemary said, "My uncle paid for his education, and, you know, that wasn't going to be the same for me, because I was a girl." Their family took the boy's education seriously and encouraged him in tangible ways. They made sacrifices to support him. Virginia Woolf, reviews the meager history of women's education in *Three Guineas* (1938). She contrasts this to the sacrifices families have traditionally made to pay into what she calls "Arthur's Education Fund," in the belief that the boys of the family are worthy of the best education the family can afford. Rosemary, like the centuries-long string of women whom Woolf summons as witnesses, did not get any such encouragement and considerably less of what Woolf called "paid-for education."

After high school Rosemary wanted to become a physical therapist. The inspiration for this came from a friend who had polio. She had watched her friend progress from "heavy iron braces" to being able to walk again. Rosemary wanted to help others through her work, and a way of doing so was made concrete and personal for her through this experience with a friend. Rosemary was accepted into a physical therapy program, but it did not start until junior year, so for her freshman and sophomore years she went to a nearby college to prepare by studying sciences. She also worked as an aide in a hospital. After two years of this program, she recognized that for her, "It was just a fantasy, doing something for someone like that." In fact, she did not like biology or the hospital work. A counselor, to whom she is grateful today, advised her to do something else. She asked herself, "What were my true loves? Government, history, literature."

She did not go on to the physical therapy program, but transferred to a Catholic college. She had to take several theology courses to make up for her two years in a secular school, and although some of it seemed to her rather abstract—"You know, how many angels dance on the head of a pin"—one course was really exciting. The professor was a former priest who had lost his position in the church, because he took part in civil rights demonstrations and was arrested. With this man as her advisor, Rosemary helped start a civil rights group in her college.

When she graduated in 1964, however, she was uncertain of what she wanted to do next. She said, "I didn't have a clue what I wanted to do. I mean it was like, you know, I didn't want to get married. And what were the choices for a woman back then? I couldn't . . . I didn't have a picture. It was a blank."

I remember at this same stage in my own life that sense of a blank, which I imagined as a curtain, a heavy, opaque one. I just could not picture any possible futures for myself. I think this was true for many women who received a middle-class education in the years before the Women's Movement. Although for some women their choices were clear and limited, others of us were unable to imagine having control over the future, choosing a goal, and going after it. After all, we had been raised with the expectation, conscious or not, that we would marry someone who would make all those decisions for us and would also give meaning to our lives.

I asked Rosemary when she decided that she did not want to get married. She said, "Well, I just didn't want to get married right after school. A lot of people just wanted to get married. I mean I had hardly dated, not much anyhow. Um, I couldn't, it's not that I decided I didn't want to, I couldn't picture it. And I think that's because my parents' marriage was so . . . difficult. You know, I couldn't imagine what that would be like."

Lucy remembered how, at this same age, she had romanticized visions of her future as a wife. Lucy thought, "If I got married and had children, I could kind of retreat from the work world and just live in a fantasy kind of world and be an artist—but it didn't work out that way at all." Rosemary, in fact, had the same limited choices held out to her, but she did not fall for the romantic vision.

Rosemary stayed at home the first year after college and got a job teaching in a junior high school. She had a very hard time. She felt she had no authority—the kids "ate her up." Her political views were another liability. She talked with her students about her strong feelings against the Vietnam War, an event that Lucy also mentioned as having affected her life. After this year Rosemary was not rehired, which was all right with her, because she wanted "to get away, to travel, to live in Europe—you know, do all these different things! I was very interested in politics and government and poverty. I wanted to understand what was going on."

Over the next few years she did do several of the things she mentioned. She worked for the Welfare Department in New York City, where she learned a lot. She spent a year teaching in Switzerland at an oppressive boarding school. At the school the students' letters home were censored, which Rosemary considered eminently unjust, so she ran an underground mail service for the students, taking their letters to the post office herself.

After that year, she moved to San Francisco where she was easily and immediately hired as a teacher, helped, as she sees it, by her background. "I had this great resume. I was Irish Catholic." Although she had no certification or master's degree, the woman who hired her, as well as "the people who ran the school system," were all Irish Catholics. Her position was "swing relief," meaning that she moved from class to class so teachers could have release time. She did this for two years, and it gave her a very broad introduction to different teaching styles and to diverse populations of students.

During this time Rosemary read Simone de Beauvoir's book *The Second Sex* (1957). The importance of this book for her, she recalls, was that it raised the possibility of "questioning the culture."

> *Rosemary:* I think in her preface there's something she wrote about being able to question the culture, and I thought, my God, here I was a history major, and I never questioned what we were doing!
> *Carla:* When did you read it?
> *Rosemary:* When I was in San Francisco, so it was the late sixties. And that book came out in the fifties. Why wasn't that book given to me in college? [Yes, me too!] That's another thing, I mean, there were a few history books written about women in the first half of the century, and as a history major, I should have had access to them. I had access to nothing! [I didn't either.]

Here we both react with anger, recalling that those ideas were out there at the time, but we didn't know it. It could be argued that, if Simone de Beauvoir's book had been placed in her hands, she might not have wanted to read it at the time. But what if the history of women had been part of history classes? Rosemary's reaction is particularly strong because she sees that even as a history major, she had never been encouraged to question the culture before. *The Second Sex* became for her "a turning point in beginning to understand what the hell happened to women." *The Second Sex* and other books Rosemary read at that time helped her to historicize women's experience and to understand how historical factors have played a part in shaping who women are and what they can do. Thus her interest in history supported her new interest in women's issues.

Rosemary recalled an anomaly that amused and puzzled her from the time she spent in San Francisco. She had a landlord who was gay—the first gay person she had ever consciously known. But even then, she said, "It never occurred to me that there were *women* who were gay," much less that she might be one of them. Rosemary relates her complete ignorance of lesbianism to the fact that she did not live in a dorm during college, but stayed at home. She felt she missed out on a lot of talk and information—"basic education," as she called it. Her ignorance is also powerful evidence of the invisibility of lesbian existence in this culture, which as Adrienne Rich (1986) points out is maintained by the overwhelming assumption that all "normal" people are heterosexual. Interestingly, this is another example of the ideas that were in the air but for various reasons not available to Rosemary at the time.

After two years, Rosemary began to feel the distance from her family and friends on the East Coast. When she came home for a vacation, she visited some friends who were teachers. They urged her to find a teaching job in their area, telling her which school districts to try for and which to avoid. That's how in 1970 she started teaching in the school system where she still works.

The town had a new superintendent who was a "change agent," in the language of the 1970s, and did not flinch when Rosemary told him that she had been reading *Teaching as a Subversive Activity, The Open Classroom, Summerhill,* and *Push Back the Desks.*[2] Like Lucy with her first teaching job, Rosemary wasn't sure she really wanted the job, so she didn't try to hide her radical ideas, and the superintendent hired her anyway.

The school to which she was assigned, however, was very conservative. All the teachers had been there "forever," and they were all natives of the area. Her experience as a new teacher is vividly captured by her description of an incident that occurred during her first year. She recalled, "I had no materials. They had taken everything out of my room and just left, you know, a set of dictionaries and some language books, and I think I had about—something like—*eight* containers of brown paint. So I sent them around to all the other teachers in the building saying, 'Would you take one brown and give me another color?' When they came back, there was one container of black paint, and the rest were still brown! Oh, it was wild."

At this point, which was early in the first interview, I noted in the transcript that we both laughed, and I had "a sense of real sharing." Curiously, I made a similar note in my first interview with Lucy, and the "real sharing" in both cases was around our early, painful experiences of teaching. Lucy, Rosemary, and I had all been hired with some unrealistic expectations (on the part of both our administrators and ourselves) of how we would manage open, change-oriented classrooms in schools that were not converted to these new educational ideas.

As Rosemary continues, her talk contains several period references:

> *Rosemary:* And then, you know, I was coming from a big city school system where people loved whatever you did, and I knew what I *didn't* want to do more than what I *did* want to do. I was reading all this stuff. This superintendent was a change agent, so there was this Education Development Center which was running workshops for teachers. I was going to them.
>
> *Carla:* So there was the superintendent up here and Rosemary down here, and there was nothing in between!
>
> *Rosemary:* Yeah, exactly, he was supporting all this stuff. And so we had this interesting math/science program and we had Tri-wall, and I had saber saws, electric saber saws, and I had drills and we were making furniture and measuring and gluing things. And I had a mattress in my reading corner.

The "change agent" superintendent encouraged work with EDC, an organization that developed innovative curriculum materials and approaches. Tri-wall was a thick cardboard material that kids could cut easily with a saw for making furniture or other items. A mattress for a cozy reading corner was a staple of the 1970s alternative classroom. And here at last we see Rosemary using and teaching with power tools.

Rosemary's next assignment was in an "overflow school" with several sixth grades housed in the basement of a parochial school. She taught in two other schools in the system and eventually made her way back to her original school, where she now teaches. She feels that the school is very supportive of her and a supportive and caring place in general. This sense of support has been particularly important to her in regard to her activism and her lesbianism.

Rosemary was active in the Women's Movement of the 1970s. For a while she belonged to a consciousness-raising group, but in her opinion it became "just a support group," where people talked about their personal problems without enough emphasis on the need for political change. She herself was "too busy being an activist," so she quit the group. She joined the National Organization for Women, worked on the Equal Rights Amendment campaign, and helped pass a state law prohibiting discrimination based on sex, race, religion, and nationality in the public schools.

One spring in the mid-1970s, she participated in the local Gay Pride March as president of her local chapter of NOW. It was fine, she recalled, because she thought she was straight. She had grown up assuming that she was heterosexual. Adrienne Rich (1986) calls this "compulsory heterosexuality," pointing out that this society shapes girls from a young age into a heterosexual mode. What people often assume is a "sexual preference" by most women is actually not a choice at all, within the strictures of a heterosexual, homophobic, and patriarchal society, but the absence of an alternative.

The summer after the Pride March, Rosemary fell in love—with a woman. The following year, she participated in the Pride March again in her capacity as NOW president, but this time, as a lesbian, she felt different, exposed and vulnerable. She was not yet out; she was afraid to be out because of her position as a teacher.

Rosemary worked for the passage of state legislation to protect gays and lesbians in the workplace. Occasionally she needed time off from school for her lobbying work, and the administration always granted it. The civil rights bill, she said, came before the legislature annually from 1973 until 1989, when it finally passed.

Without the protection of this state law, Rosemary would not have felt that she could come out in her school. "I knew I had no legal rights until the gay rights bill passed in 1989. I thought it would be foolish to come out, you know, because if someone made a big deal of it, I would be in trouble."

For years she was closeted in school, her reality known only to one colleague. When that colleague moved away, Rosemary said poignantly, she was left "without anyone in the school system that I was authentic with." She figured some people concluded that she was a lesbian merely from her active involvement in the Women's Movement—referring again, as she did in our first conversation, to the assumption some people make that feminists are lesbians. She was prevented from coming out to her colleagues or being "authentic" with them by what she called a "wall of fear."

After the passage of the bill, Rosemary began to talk more openly with some of her fellow teachers. During this time, when some knew and some didn't know that she was a lesbian, she said, "I'd sit at lunch, and every once in a while someone might make a comment about gays. Then I'd feel like a jerk for not saying anything, but I wouldn't want to embarrass someone in front of the whole group, so the assistant principal would take the person aside and talk to them about what they said." Short of outing Rosemary, the assistant principal would talk to the person who had made the offensive remark about the importance of respecting differences in the school. But now, Rosemary pointed out, "That doesn't happen any more."

Prior to coming out, Rosemary had garnered the three kinds of support that she thought she needed: legal, institutional, and personal. In coming out to her school, it helped that she had taught in the same town for nearly twenty years and was well known to her colleagues. She had been active in her own school and had served as vice president of the local teachers' union. She also built her support through her work on the Diversity Committee, which included teachers and administrators from other schools in the system. Because of these varied connections, she felt, her colleagues did not see her only as a lesbian, but rather as a person known and respected who is a lesbian. Her lesbianism is an aspect of her, and one that they appear at least to accept.

As it happened, however, she came out to her students before she came out to the faculty as a group. In the spring of 1993, at a raffle for the Parent-Teacher Organization, she won a free airline ticket. She used this PTO windfall to fly to Washington and participate in the March on Washington for Lesbian, Gay, and Bisexual Equal Rights and Liberation. She missed a day of school, and on her return, her students, curious about her absence, spoke to her. What follows is the story in her words:

> *Rosemary:* The kids were saying, "We know where you were. You were in Washington." And I'm like changing the subject, and finally one boy after school says, "I *know* you were in Washington." I said, "You're right." So then I thought, How shall I do this? Because I wanted to come out to my class, and I wanted to do it right. So I asked two high school teachers I know and a friend who's an elementary teacher at a private school. They said, "Be positive. Don't start with discrimination. Start with celebrating differences."
>
> So I kept that in mind, and later on in the spring I went to the local Gay Pride March, and I decided to tell my kids about that. In class on Monday we do this thing, What Did You Do on the Weekend? And everyone talks about their weekend. I said, "I had an interesting weekend. I had a great time. I went to the Gay Pride March. There were gay and straight students and teachers from lots of high schools. I went to a party where there were lesbian and gay teachers." And I said, "The Saturday before I was at the state Department of Ed being trained, you know, so I could train teachers to make the schools safe for gay and lesbian students." And they spoke as a group—and you can see I don't run my class where they speak as a group—and they spoke as a group, and they said, "That's good, Ms. Trowbridge," and they applauded. I just coulda died.

Later that morning she took the class out to recess,

> And three girls called me over, and I know they're going to ask me the question, 'cause I didn't say, "I am a lesbian." And this was hysterical, 'cause there's this one girl, Rachel—her mother was a teacher, and I think she was always empowered. She saw herself as my assistant. So she called me over. She said, "I have to ask you a question about what you said this morning." This other girl, Becky, you know, she was an artist, she was going, "Don't ask! Don't ask!" And Rachel was going, "I just have to ask." So she said, "Are you a ___ ? Are you a ___?" And she couldn't say *lesbian*, so I said, "Lesbian?" And she said, "Yes!" And I said, "Yes, that's what I was telling you this morning." So Becky was going, "It's OK! It's OK! It's OK!" And little Kate, who's

like my right-hand person—she always knew where everything was in my desk—was bending over going, "Ouhh! It's disgusting! You do that?"—like she was going to vomit. And I said, "Kate, all it means is, if you're straight you fall in love with someone of the opposite gender, and if you're gay you fall in love with someone of the same gender. That's all it means, and I'm still your teacher. You still have to do your homework."

So they went off to play. End of the day. Becky [of "Don't ask, don't tell"] comes over and says [stage whisper], "You know what you said this morning?" I said, "Yes." [laughing] "Well, Kate [of "Oh, it's disgusting"] has told the whole school at lunch. Now everybody knows." And I said, "Oh, good, that's why I told you." And that was the end of it.

There were no further comments from the kids that year. Life did go on, as Rosemary had warned, with her apt mention of homework as one of the constants of life. But that was not the end of it. The following September the acting principal and acting assistant principal asked Rosemary to speak to the whole faculty and explain to them why she had come out to her class. These two acting administrators were in charge of the school for only two months at the beginning of the year. They wanted to support and protect Rosemary, and they wanted the other teachers' questions answered. "They came to me, and they said, 'We want to put you on the faculty meeting. We want you to tell the whole school why you came out, why it's important, and we need every faculty member behind you, because parents are more likely to go talk to them than to you, so we want you to explain to them so everyone's with you.'"

Rosemary was glad of this opportunity. It was, nevertheless, "the most difficult thing I've ever done. You totally expose yourself to whatever people think. Whatever ideas they have, they take you and compare you to those ideas."

As will be made clear in the classroom section, Rosemary had in a sense been preparing her students all year by discussing prejudice and discrimination against many groups, including lesbians and gays. By the spring, she had a good sense of how her students saw these issues and what they were ready for.

But she had not talked about these issues with many members of the faculty. She did not know what they thought, and she feared the worst. She felt terribly vulnerable, knowing how "They take you and compare you to those ideas." So at the faculty meeting she spoke of some of these ideas, or stereotypes, telling them how she knew that many people think of lesbians as child molesters and how painful that was to her. She talked frankly of her fears and her sense of isolation. She felt that her colleagues were able to see how painful her experience had been, and how some of their biases were up for reexamination.

In this clash between a known person and a set of ideas not previously associated with that person, Rosemary felt she turned matters around. Instead of feeling herself being compared to their preexisting ideas, she forced her colleagues to hold up their prejudices and stereotypes against what they already knew about her as a human being and as a colleague. In other words, they had to look not only at Rosemary but at their own ideas. Learning about her suffering, she thought, shook them up so that they realized, "Oh, I hadn't thought about it that way," which can be the beginning of awareness.

As Rosemary described the event, "It was very emotional. I just started crying when I got up, and the acting principal—I've known this man for a long time, and I just love him—he put his arm around me while I talked. And I'm crying and talking, and finally I'm on my own two feet, and by the time I finished, *he* was crying. I mean, it was just a very—it was very powerful, but, I mean, it's just a wonderful, wonderful group of people."

Rosemary had not expected to end up crying, and she thinks she surprised her colleagues too. People saw her as strong, an activist whom they had read about in the newspaper. Now here she was in front of them, crying. "After I spoke to the faculty meeting the first time in September, maybe there were five people out of the whole group who *didn't* come up and put their arm around me and tell me that I was terrific and how they were so proud of me."

The acceptance Rosemary felt on that occasion and subsequently has contributed to her sense of this school as a supportive and caring place. On the other hand, she finds she still needs to work on the awareness of her colleagues and remind them that she is a lesbian. One day several teachers were discussing a colleague who they felt was too demonstrative with her kindergarten class. Rosemary also felt that her behavior—holding and carrying her children—was "inappropriate." The other teachers said, "If it was a male teacher, he'd be up on charges." Rosemary added, "'Yeah, and if I did that *I'd* be up on charges'—and people looked at me like, '*Huh?* Oh, yeah, right.' [laughter] They had to make a connection, like why would I be up on charges? It took them a little while."

In jokes and stories and conversation, Rosemary reminds her colleagues of her different positioning. "And I do it on purpose. I want to remind them that there's a difference, like, so what? And just to tease them, because I know the other side, people hearing jokes and teasing, so I want to tease them." As a way to maintain her authenticity with her colleagues, and also to increase their awareness, Rosemary uses jokes and teasing so that they will know something of "the other side."

Although she consistently presented her colleagues in very warm and grateful terms, I couldn't help but wonder myself what it meant to the staff to accept her as a lesbian. Many of them, Rosemary noted, were

Catholics. One day at lunch in the teachers' room, the talk started with stories of lost objects, then moved on to St. Anthony and the efficacy of prayer. Those who spoke sounded to me like practicing Catholics. In their conversation, appearance, dress, and manner, the faculty struck me as somewhat conservative. My bias was that these characteristics would make it harder for her colleagues to accept this new knowledge about Rosemary. I asked her if she ever felt hostility or reserve from them. She responded with another story:

> *Rosemary:* I think I—no, I think what happens is that people like me as a person, and then they have their prejudice. I'll give you an example. Ruth, who teaches second grade, is new in the school this year, but she's been in the system. We know *of* each other; we don't really know each other. She's very Catholic, you know, very involved in her church. Several years ago, she was on the Diversity Committee when we first came together as a system-wide committee. We had a full-day workshop. We had a facilitator, and we're doing this getting-to-know-you activity, and it's like, I don't know what the directions were, but something like, "Tell someone something about yourself that, I don't know, you usually don't tell or you're afraid to tell." Ruth's in front of me. I say, "Ruth, I'm a lesbian." She says, "I knew that." Just like that. It was like, *"Next!"* [laughter]
>
> OK, so then the next year she doesn't come to any of the meetings of the Diversity Committee. She doesn't come to meetings, has no idea what went on. She comes this year. She shows up for the second meeting. I'm there, and she says, "Oh, I just have to tell you . . ." You know, she dominates the meeting with this story which goes on and on and on—that she was walking through the high school to come to the meeting, and someone said to her, "Where are you going, Ruth? What are you doing in the high school?" And she said, "Oh, I'm going to the Diversity meeting." And the person said, [dry voice] "Oh, you're going to *that* meeting?" That's all they said to her, and she came upstairs and said, "Know what happened to me? Well, people just think that this is—that all we talk about is the issue of homosexuals or gays and lesbians"—however she said it. Now, that person never said that. That's *Ruth* saying that. And there's the perception—that's all we talk about, you know—so *she* is really uncomfortable with this.

The level of awareness and the level of acceptance vary among Rosemary's colleagues. Her work to raise those levels is a large and long-term undertaking. In a conversation a year later, Rosemary told me about overhearing a hallway conversation that pleased her. One kid yelled at another, "You fag!" A teacher spoke to him, "We don't use those words in school." A second teacher, who was passing by added, "We don't use those words—period."

Soon after her first appearance before the faculty, Rosemary's administrators asked her to talk with the faculty again. They wanted her to tell teachers what they could do to make their classrooms safe for gay and lesbian students. In Rosemary's opinion, at that time (the early 1990s) this was not happening in other public elementary schools. She spoke passionately of the importance of this work:

> *Rosemary:* And the thing is, I can't tell you how many people have come to me and said, "My nephew, my daughter, you know, our best friend." So many people have stories, and they've had no one to talk to. And then they have to know that, if all this violence and suicide is going to stop, you know, we have to start breaking the silence. We can't start unteaching prejudice in the middle school. They're so insecure and like off the wall at that age anyhow. And you know, people at my school *get it* that you start teaching people to care for each other as soon as you get them in your class. You don't wait till they're fourteen or fifteen.

In coming out at school, as in her political work, Rosemary has found a voice with which to express who she is—the "authentic" self she had hidden for years—and where she stands on causes that she feels are important. But the effort to speak with that authentic voice is an ongoing struggle. Rosemary reminded me of this when we were talking about a gender workshop in which we had both felt silenced. This painful event seemed to both of us a throwback, a moment of defeat in a long struggle. It also became part of our common history—an event we kept referring back to, as Lucy and I kept referring to the *stamina* episode.

Rosemary asked if I would like to go with her to a workshop on Gender Issues in the Classroom. It was one of those in-service days when the kids race through a half day at school on fast-forward, then depart, while the exhausted teachers hurry off to another building to attend workshops with other teachers from across the system.

There were about eight elementary and fifteen secondary people in our workshop, both teachers and administrators. Four of the company were men. The workshop leader, Rose, was an experienced speaker who worked out of a nearby research center. She began with a summary of recent findings on girls in education. She invited people to ask questions. Two or three women spoke, one of whom claimed that boys have a harder time of it in school than girls. Two of the men were silent; the other two men, who turned out to be brothers, dominated. One of the brothers taught kindergarten. He gave a long, emotional speech on how gender issues are *not* the problem; "family issues" are. We don't know how bad it's going to get, he said, or what he has to put up with at K level. The woman who thought boys suffer more asked him to give examples, and, with such encouragement, he did, at great length—effectively undercutting Rose's workshop.

After he had carried on for a while, Rose finally said, "Yes, these are problems, but so are gender issues, which is what we're here for today." Even this did not shut him up. He said that it's different here in this town where most of the school administrators are women. Rose tried to counter with issues of what women face once they do get into positions of power.

His brother, who teaches social studies at the high school, was similarly ponderous. He also emphasized that there's no problem in this town, but for a different reason. Parents send their sons to private schools, if they can afford it (Arthur's Education Fund again)—but not their daughters, which he did *not* point out—and, therefore, there are equal numbers of girls in advanced science and math courses, and some of the top students are girls!

We broke into (I wish I could say laughter) small groups for a different activity. Rosemary and I were feeling the effects of those two men, as were all the women in the two elementary groups, but in our small group, we went on with the agenda and didn't talk directly about what had happened. In the other elementary group, the K teacher completely dominated the conversation with two other teachers and a principal. Then he walked out early.

At the end of the workshop there were women in knots, asking ourselves, "What just happened? What have we been through? Why haven't we acted?" Rosemary and I had a long *cafe latte,* while we went over the workshop: the redefining of issues, the question of power, the ways in which these issues were "not a problem" in this town, our own smoldering reactions. We were caught off guard by this event, which was for both of us an example of silencing, of frustration, of self-accusation, of internalized oppression, of not being able to carry our ideas into practice.

During the workshop, the reactions on both sides seemed antediluvian. They were so like those that came up in the first sexism workshops I led in the early 1970s. Some things have changed, but there are still things we do not seem to have gotten past. I had thought that there were arguments that even chauvinists would not make in public anymore. I had thought that by now feminists would be able to counter such arguments effectively. But the battle goes on. A colleague—a tough woman, a fighter—who read an account of this workshop wrote in the margin, "I know these feelings so well!" The afternoon left both Rosemary and me with all too familiar feelings of guilt, rage, and disbelief.

Rosemary also told me about a TV appearance she had made a few years ago. When she saw the video afterward, she liked what she had said, but she was appalled to observe that she had kept her eyes lowered during the entire interview—even as she said some pretty radical things. A friend told her that she was still being "the good, demure Catholic girl." With that knowledge, in her next TV appearance, Rosemary looked the camera smack in the eye.

An important theme in Rosemary's life, as she recounted it to me, has been her longing "just to be a whole person and, you know, not to pass." She has had to struggle to live who she is in her work and to express who she is through her teaching and political activism. The fact that this struggle is so important in her life influences her classroom practice in many ways.

ROSEMARY'S CLASSROOM

You don't get the full flavor of Sumner School if you arrive, as I did, by the side street that leads to the elementary wing. The original part of this building is a crenellated extravaganza that was once the high school. It sits surrounded by playgrounds, which are in turn surrounded by neat, small, single family houses. Most of this older building was given over from pedagogical to entrepreneurial purposes when a new high school was built in another part of town. The auditorium is still used—a murky, echoey room, where I witnessed the Veterans Day ceremonies with Rosemary's class. A long, thin, unheated structure makes a link to the building that holds the elementary classrooms.

The elementary building has straight corridors with green and white tiles on the floor and rectangular rooms. The corridors are lined with lockers and covered with children's art, with cautionary and informative posters, and with commercial artwork. Entering the school for the first time, I felt that the result of all this decoration would not quite succeed in suggesting cheerfulness and warmth—assuming that was its intent—if the people had not been so friendly. Everyone I passed smiled and said "hello."

As I walked down the long corridor, the school looked, smelled, and sounded exactly like the elementary school I had attended many years ago. This added to my impression of a somewhat traditional and conservative school. In fact, as I later found, there are many efforts going on that attempt to break down that rectilinear separation of individuals and groups—and to create a more caring community against the underlying geometry of straight lines and right angles.

The school holds 644 children, in kindergarten through grade five. Most of the students arrive at school by bus. The population is made up of numerous ethnic groups—Armenian, Greek, Iranian, Irish, Italian, and Turkish, among others. Some of these groups maintained a strong cultural identity within the larger community.

Most of the families are working class or middle class. Rosemary mentioned various jobs held by her students' parents: accountant, psychologist, nurse, teacher's aide, police officer, clerk, writer, and housecleaner.

There were also mothers and fathers who did not work but stayed at home. Some were out of work or doing temp work or were on welfare. Some had disabilities.

Rosemary's fifth grade class had thirteen boys and nine girls. Her room was a large box, with the traditionally assigned uses of the four walls: one window wall, one chalkboard wall, one bulletin board wall, and the wall with the door that has a window, allowing surveillance from the hall. A rabbit, P. J., who ran loose in the room, added an antic note. Rosemary had her desk at the front. The children's desks were in a semicircle, with four desks forming an island in the center. The desks were moved two times during the period of my data collection. Rosemary planned the desk arrangements and assigned seats. An additional spatial factor she needed to consider was that one of the children, Leonard, had cerebral palsy and for most of the time was confined to a wheelchair.

Rosemary's desk was heaped with stuff, as were most other horizontal surfaces in the room. The walls were covered with kids' work, and the tables held numerous projects in various stages of completion. The clutter seemed relaxed, comfortable, kid-centered, not out of control. There was a lectern, where the children stood when they read or talked to the class, an easel with a flip chart that presented the day's schedule, a revolving bookcase full of paperbacks, and several bins containing math materials.

Unlike Lucy, Rosemary did not have a printed schedule for each day of the week. The days of the week were relatively meaningless in her school anyway. They had been renamed *A, B, C, D, E,* and *F.* This logistic nightmare was the result of a budget cut that made it necessary for the specialists to hold their classes only every sixth day, instead of every fifth. The teachers were inured to the system and only gave it an occasional sarcastic remark. Whenever Rosemary and I tried to do any planning, she would bring out her school schedule and say, "Oh, no, sorry, that is *E* Day; we'll be having gym." In this elementary school classroom, as in Lucy's and many others', it seems to be the specialists' schedule (and the consequent release time for the classroom teacher) that largely determines the classroom schedule. In addition, there are the schedules of reading aides, speech therapists, band, special projects, and other events. Classroom teachers sometimes feel they have to make do with what's left over.

Each day Rosemary wrote her plans on the flip chart and discussed them with the kids. The plans were very flexible, and she always planned too much. At the end of the day she would look at the schedule, sigh, cross out the things that they had accomplished and move the rest to the next day.

In the following four sections, I discuss what I saw going on in Rosemary's classroom. Each section connects what I had learned about Rosemary—about who she is—with what I observed in her room and with what she and I had to say about it in our discussions. The first section discusses Rosemary's long-term interest in questioning the dominant culture and shows how she uses this critical stance to help her students raise questions and deal with the world. The next describes specific practices Rosemary employs in dealing with differences in her classroom. In the third section I discuss how Rosemary's position as a lesbian and an activist influences her work in the classroom, and in the fourth I show various ways in which she uses her position as a teacher to empower her students.

Questioning the Culture

As Rosemary talked about her life, she said, "I've always been very political." She connected her own interest in history and politics with her family's interest and the talk at home as she was growing up. She said her parents saw politics as "a way to create fairness." Later, after she read *The Second Sex*, she began to see how feminism, through the questions it asks about the world, could lead to "questioning the culture" in a way she had not done before. Now as a teacher she makes sure that her students are aware of what is going on in the world and that they begin to question the culture—particularly its sexist, homophobic, racist, and classist aspects.

Sometimes Rosemary helped her students extend their awareness of current issues through the books they read. In the period before Christmas, Tina brought in an illustrated book of Hans Christian Andersen's *The Little Matchgirl*, the story of a poor, starving orphan who sells matches on a city street. Tina wanted to read the fairytale to the class, which Rosemary let her do during snack time. Except for the crunch of potato chips and the scraping of chairs, the kids were very quiet and attentive listening to this classic children's tale. When the reading was over, Rosemary asked for responses to the book, and then, rather than leaving this story in the nineteenth century amidst the horrors of the Industrial Revolution, she moved the discussion on to the problems of homelessness today and how the children's own town was affected. They learned that there were homeless children in their school, a fact that might otherwise have escaped them.

When Rosemary and her class did a unit on Native American people, she did not use the dog-eared copies of the fifth grade social studies text. "I mean, whose story is in it?" she asked disparagingly, meaning that the books that stayed on the shelf told only the story of the conquerors. In order to get a range of perspectives, she told the children to choose books for themselves at the town library, and in class they discussed the different ways Native Americans were portrayed. She also showed several movies, one of which presented a mixed picture of the current life of two

Native American communities. There were some positive scenes—traditional gatherings, classes with children eagerly learning their native language and listening to stories. These scenes, however, were placed against a background of poverty, unemployment, and alcoholism. Afterward, Rosemary asked the children for their reactions, and they mentioned various things that struck them: how the unfair housing arrangements kept the native people in poverty, what limited opportunities they had, how many died young. Then Rosemary asked what the children thought was the purpose of the movie. These answers were abbreviated in my notes:

> *Heather:* So we would treat them better.
> *Betsy:* To show they're not as bad as we've thought.
> *Terry:* [Some of this I couldn't hear.] We killed a lot of Indians.
> *Laurie:* To show how life was then.
> *Lydia:* We have running water, heat—we think that's the way life is, but it's not.

With the possible exception of Laurie, who seems to think this movie takes place in the past, the children here are questioning some of their received notions about American Indians. Lydia took a further step, an impressive step for a ten-year-old, using what she had learned about Native Americans to reflect on her own assumptions about life.

In teaching the school curriculum, Rosemary reached beyond the school's texts in order to challenge the stereotypical White ideas of American Indians, either negative or highly romanticized, that are passed on in this society and often in schools. She presented Native Americans as people of today who have many strengths and also many problems, which are not so far removed from some of the problems the children in Rosemary's class also face.

Rosemary took an approach to current events that provided her with insight into her students' thinking and their concerns about the wider society. She did not use a packaged children's newspaper, but asked her students to bring in articles from grown-up newspapers and magazines once a week. They were to read the articles carefully beforehand so they could summarize them to their classmates. When they did this, they stood at the lectern with the article in front of them.

On one occasion, Henry told about a little boy who shot his brother while playing with a handgun. Tina reported on White teenagers throwing stones at a seven-year-old Black child. Raymond told about a study of air pollution in six communities (including their own) that related pollution to increased death rates. Terry told about women who were battered—"battered women and AIDS," she said. Actually the article was about legislation that aids battered women. Rosemary asked her to reread it and bring it in again Monday. Betsy reported on a man who attempted to kidnap a student at a school in a nearby town.

On another occasion the articles were about domestic violence in the military and a burned cross that had been found in the city. These were all violent and frightening stories, but they were the means for bringing crucial issues into the classroom, where these fifth graders could think about them and share their reactions with their friends and teacher. In Rosemary's classroom they were relatively safe, but they were not isolated from the rest of the world, not shut up in their brick rectangle. Their teacher helped them to make connections with the outside world, and by discussing some of its harsher aspects in the classroom circle, she might have helped her kids to deal with them.

I envied Rosemary's students their position in this class located in the world. My experience of elementary school was that the walls of the building *did* shut out the world. I was not helped to connect what I learned inside with what I knew or wondered about outside. And much that was happening outside was never recognized inside. An important theme in Madeleine Grumet's *Bitter Milk* is the need for teachers to create in their classrooms what she variously calls a "real space in the middle (20) and a "safe place" (90). Grumet conceives of this as a space that mediates between the private world of home and the broader public world, between maternal nurturance and the patriarchal order. Rosemary creates this kind of space in her classroom, where her students can feel safe while they are thinking and acting in ways that could help prepare them for the world outside, the world beyond and after school.

Rosemary herself felt that her constant discussions of political issues with the children and their heightened awareness of bias, discrimination, and hate crimes made it possible for last year's class to be so accepting and supportive when she finally came out to them. In fact, she had created a "safe place" for herself as well.

Dealing with Differences

Rosemary believes that the fact that she is a lesbian makes her particularly sensitive to issues of prejudice and intolerance. "I know the other side, people hearing jokes and teasing." She feels this knowledge has contributed to a sense of safety in her classroom. "And you know what? It creates safety. No one can hurt anyone else, and it breaks down gender roles." She quoted a fellow teacher to illustrate this sense of safety:

> *Rosemary:* And that's what Betty had said to me—this woman who's out at a private school. She's been out for a couple of years. She's a fifth grade teacher. She said she can see that the gender roles break down, that it's OK to be who you are, and, you know, girls don't *have* to be a certain way. Boys

don't *have* to be a certain way. You can be who you are. And she has a phrase which I think is wonderful that—in terms of gender roles, never mind in terms of homophobia—there are a million little suicides that happen—like you know, "I can't join chorus because I'm a boy." You censor yourself because of gender roles, and I think that that dissipates [when people are able and allowed to be who they are].

Rosemary gave an example of the "breaking down of gender roles" from last year's class. The class was discussing what to do for fifth grade graduation. Usually, she said, one kid from each class would get up and give "some boring little speech." Rosemary wanted to do something more interesting and something that would involve more of her students. She was pleased when one of them, a boy, suggested, "Let's say thank you to music!"

> *Rosemary:* And when it was over every boy and girl in my class was on that stage dancing in front of all the parents of the fifth grade. Now that's amazing! And the boys—now the girls, yes, and a few boys—but for *everybody* to be on that stage—and I know it's because it's safe to be who you are here, and you can be anything you want. And I think part of that is me being a lesbian and they knowing it and, so what? It's like anything is OK, everyone is OK.

This loosening of narrowly defined gender roles seemed to me evident on my first visit to Rosemary's classroom. The class had just finished reading *Matilda* by Roald Dahl. Rosemary told me it was a favorite book of theirs—and hers. Intricate, carefully drawn illustrations that the children had made from the book decorated one wall. The kids were currently working in small groups on skits of various scenes from the book. All the groups had both girls and boys in them. As they practiced their skits, they seemed very involved and amicable. Later they came up group by group to show their skits to Rosemary and me, where we sat at the side of the room.

The major roles in *Matilda* are all female—Matilda herself, a powerful little girl; her teacher, Miss Honey; and the school head, Miss Trunchbull. Their names say it all. Miss Honey is gentle and of course sweet; Miss Trunchbull is a monster.[3] In several cases, boys took the female parts, but there wasn't a hint of apology as they introduced their characters or any apparent awkwardness when they performed for us. During the whole project, Rosemary said, no boy had complained about having to play a female part. This behavior contrasts with what I had observed in Lucy's classroom, where the separation between boys and girls and the taboos related to what boys and girls could do seemed so important to those second graders. It also contrasts with what Barrie Thorne found in the fourth and fifth grade classrooms she researched for *Gender Play*. There, the separation between girls and boys was maintained by mutual avoidance, rivalry, teasing, insults, and stereotyping.

Rosemary consciously structures this safe place where, for example, boys can play female characters without embarrassment. She fights to prevent those "million little suicides" in several ways. I discuss five of them in what follows.

1. *Discussion.* The most pervasive structure that supported Rosemary's safe place was the ongoing class discussion of issues of difference, of which I have already given some examples. A great many of these issues were brought in from the news and outside sources, as mentioned previously, and kids knew that prejudicial remarks of their own would lead to further discussion. While I was there, I never heard an explicitly sexist or homophobic remark from any of the children.

Rosemary brought up the issue of race frequently. There were no children of color in Rosemary's class, and very few in the school as a whole, but, as she was aware, the issue was still present in the classroom. Sometimes the children brought in articles that dealt with racial issues, and, as Rosemary points out, they then had the opportunity to deal with racism in the reporting of the news as well.

Rosemary: We also talk about the news, because I think you can get a really racist view of what's going on. Oh, it's those Black people who are so violent, you know. And I noticed Laurie said something the other day about some violence in town, and she prefaced it by saying it was a Black man, you know. We don't bother to say it's a White man but she prefaced it by saying he was Black, so I've been thinking about what I'm going to do about that. I didn't say anything right then, but—'cause I wasn't sure exactly what to say.

I thought that was a subtle point for a kid, especially since most White adults would have to have pointed out to them the underlying racism in this distinction. Unfortunately, it was a long time before I asked Rosemary what she had said to Laurie, and by then she had forgotten exactly what she did say. It seems safe to assume, however, that Rosemary does not often let such statements go unquestioned—a great temptation in any classroom where there are already too many demands and pressures—but instead sees them as opportunities to raise important questions.

2. *Seating and Groups.* Rosemary makes sure that the children sit in groups composed of both girls and boys, because, she says,

Rosemary: I hate sex role stereotyping. I hate that boys don't want to do things with girls. They don't want to sit next to them. They don't want to play with them. So I've always made girls and boys sit together. In a way they really want to, but they can't admit it. So I take that on. I'm the "baddy." I'm making you do this. I always control the seating, and I always have boys and girls sitting together, working together, I mean not exclusively but I want them to know each other as individuals and not—oh, you're a this or you're a that. I think that's always been part of who I am as a feminist—that it shouldn't make any difference, and if you like someone or dislike them, it's gonna be for, you know, their personality. It's not gonna be because of their gender.

She gives the children some choice in seating whenever they move their desks. They list two boys and two girls whom they would like to sit with. With these lists Rosemary arranges the groups so the children get at least one of their choices and, as the "baddy," she ensures that all groups are gender-mixed. Of course, there are other considerations as well, such as placing at least one good reader in each group.

The children have come to expect to have both girls and boys in all their groups. One day when a visitor led the children in some drama games, the groups were not all mixed. The boys complained, and Henry muttered discontentedly, "There are no girls in this group!"

3. *Recess.* Another way Rosemary created safety for students was structuring recess to avoid the wide separation of boys' and girls' activities that Thorne (1993) describes. Rosemary got some of these ideas from a student teacher—a source that some teachers might not acknowledge so willingly.

Rosemary: I had a student teacher once—a guy—who taught me about recess. I had never really paid attention to recess. He taught me about organized games, which I don't do all the time, but when I do they're very controlled in terms of fairness, you know, that the boys don't dominate. It's girl-boy-girl-boy. They take turns kicking; they take turns pitching; they take turns who's captain, and if kids aren't good at things—and usually most boys have more skills—we'll collect all the balls, and the kids who are skilled teach the other kids, so they can all feel kind of good about it and be able to play and have a nice game. You don't want them to insult each other, which some kids like to do. I learned how important it was for boys and girls to feel physically capable—that they could run around, have a good time, and be part of the team. And he taught me that—that's really important, so I'm very aware of it.

Carla: How did he teach you? Just by pointing out what you could do?

Rosemary: Yeah, he did it. He set it up for me, and we talked about it. I just hadn't really paid much attention to recess. And there are always boys too, you know, one or two who don't have skills and feel really stupid and uncomfortable in their bodies. You know, it cuts both ways. And there are kids who want to dominate, and because they want to dominate so much, they have no friends, and they need that social skill of being the coach instead of being the star, so there are just so many things that come out of that kind of recess.

This vision of a recess that is supportive and empowering hits many of the themes Rosemary emphasizes in her teaching—fairness, collaboration, acceptance of differences, "being the coach instead of the star." Recess is a very important part of a child's schooling, but often aides are in charge and teachers miss this opportunity to teach and learn about their students. Rosemary's school did not have aides at morning recess, and she was the only one of the three teachers I worked with who regularly went out with her kids.

Actually, I never saw a recess that was organized in the way Rosemary describes. When I was there for recess, Rosemary and I spent the time watching the kids and talking (which may be why she did not have organized games). There was usually a small group of boys in the outer field, playing ball. Many of the children did play together on an elaborate playground structure. Their roles were sometimes differentiated by gender, however. One morning a group of boys went down a steep slide, while a group of girls hung on to the side and whopped them as they came down, both girls and boys yelling and laughing. Rosemary called the girls the "gatekeepers." Occasionally she would shoo them off and tell them to go down the slide themselves.

4. *Alternation.* Like Lucy and Marcia, Rosemary was aware of the research on how boys dominate the airtime in schools, and she tried to compensate for it. Her intention was to alternate between boys and girls when she called on the children for answers.

In fact, all three case-study teachers honored the principle of girl/boy alternation, and all three were inconsistent in their practice. Life in the classroom seems just too complicated for any absolute rule of alternation. There are so many other factors—children who constantly speak out, a quiet child who finally has something to say, a child who has special knowledge or a special need to talk at that moment, a class where there are significantly more boys or more girls, an occasion when the teacher simply isn't paying attention to this issue. Then there is the profound fact of our own socialization and how it distorts our perceptions so that a roughly equal distribution of airtime in class feels like favoring the girls. Dale Spender (1982) noticed this when she videotaped classrooms, as did the Sadkers (1994). In Lucy's classroom it took me a while to recognize the underlying inequity in the discussion of Rosie and Dolores's story. The issue, which, on the face of it, seems fairly simple and quantifiable, turns out to be a great challenge for teachers who are struggling to achieve fairness in their classrooms.

In Rosemary's class, and as we will see later in Marcia's, the children were often the ones who would insist on alternating between the boys and the girls.

Rosemary: Now I always call on boy-girl-boy-girl, but sometimes I call on two boys and two girls, but this class is so vocal, "You called on two boys!" [laughter] And then they complained to me about the sub today—because I had a math day on Friday—that the sub, you know, did this for the boys and that for the boys. I asked them, "Did you say something to the sub?" They turned her in to the assistant principal! And he said to the kids, "You should speak to her—tell the sub." So they did, and she told them they were over-reacting—but I mean lots of times people don't realize it.

And some of the boys don't get it either, because as long as they're getting what they need, they don't notice anything is wrong. I mean, it's funny. The kids are aware of it. We talk about it.

In this situation, the kids took a protest into their own hands. Their familiarity with these issues made them feel empowered enough to criticize the sub and to talk to the principal about it. Unfortunately, they were put off with a line that is all too familiar to any feminist as well as to other protesting groups: "You're overreacting."

5. *Countering Stereotypes.* Rosemary encouraged the girls to be more assertive. On one occasion, when the children were reporting on books that they had found for the Indian unit, two of the girls spoke in very low voices. "Come on," Rosemary said, "be Trunchbull!" The girls laughed and tried harder. Another time Rosemary moved to stand near Rachel to help her speak to the class. She did not always wait for students to volunteer but insisted that they participate and respond.

Rosemary: I think what happens is the more you call on people who never volunteer, then they begin to volunteer. I don't know if they're any more comfortable, or if they know they're going to be called on anyhow, but I think you do build up people's confidence and self-esteem so they're not hiding so much. With *Matilda* and with the *BFG*—especially *Matilda*—they were all dying to read their part out loud because they loved it, so you know, I think they get over that hump.

I asked Rosemary how she worked to counter stereotypical behavior in boys too.

Rosemary: Well, I think, now I don't know specifically what I do about that, except the only like conscious thing I can think of is—um—encouraging boys to go down to the kindergarten, you know, and help with the little kids and help with the younger kids in gym. And they seem to like that—and the girls like it too, but the first people I would always ask to do that would be the boys. So that's one conscious thing that I would do.

Several boys left the class to help in kindergarten one frigid day when they had an indoor recess, even though there were several entertaining games and activities going on in the classroom. Rosemary continues:

> *Rosemary:* In the gender workshop you said, what about encouraging boys to listen, you know? I think that's really true, and how do you do that consciously, besides just by making everyone have a turn and force the listening on people, right? And sometimes with someone like Henry, I'll say, "You know, Henry, there are twenty-two people in here. Everyone hasn't had a chance to speak," and it's like, "Oh!" you know? So I don't know. How do you do it, by just reminding them that everyone needs a chance? But I mean I don't know. How do you do that?

Later I thought of one thing I had tried that seemed to work. I required the kids who were participating in a discussion to summarize what the previous speaker had said before adding their own ideas. Rosemary wrote herself a note about that and said she wanted to try it. She also mentioned recess in the context of this question about boys:

> *Rosemary:* I think at recess sometimes when we play organized games, and people have to take turns and aren't allowed to dominate because they're like the best athlete or, you know, they just want to win the game. I mean, I organize the game so it doesn't work that way, and we talk about it, but that's the most conscious thing I think I do.

The foregoing were some of the ways that Rosemary tried to create a classroom in which the children would get to know each other and to learn from each other's differences. By encouraging discussion, arranging seating groups, organizing recess, alternating speakers (in principle at least), and countering stereotypes, Rosemary worked to deal with the differences in her classroom by controlling the atmosphere in which these differences were played out. None of her strategies worked perfectly, but all involved vigorous effort and a lot of talking. She also gave the children wide-ranging freedom in discussing other issues that came up in class or were brought in from outside.

Questions of how we live together in a classroom—how we respect and understand and care for each other—are always part of the curriculum, although too often they are part of the "hidden curriculum" of ideas that are conveyed unconsciously by the teacher and other students. In Rosemary's room these issues were constantly in front of the kids. They could not be in that classroom for long without coming up against them. One fact underlies all of Rosemary's strategies, and it could be a crucial element in creating the feeling of comfort and safety that is in her room: The students knew without question that these issues were of vital importance to their teacher.

This year's holiday party made Rosemary particularly happy, because she believed her kids showed the sensitivity toward each other that she strove to foster. At first, as she described the party, "It bombed, the kids were bored." Then Heather wanted to read the class a newspaper clipping she had brought in about a girl with cerebral palsy. It gave rise to some questions that they asked Leonard, the boy with cerebral palsy, about what he could or couldn't do. Leonard said, "I can't walk, but I can dance. Do you want to see me dance?" Rosemary started to say, "Well maybe it's time to go on." But Leonard insisted, "No, wait, how many want to see me dance?" Some hands were raised, so he reached for his crutches and pulled himself out of his wheelchair. Somebody put on the music, and he danced. So did some other kids, and a couple of the girls danced with him.

Later Ricky wanted to read to the class from a book Rosemary had given him on divorce, because that's what he and his parents were going through. He read a chapter called "Weekend Santa," and the kids were, as Rosemary said, "mesmerized." "So that was a great Christmas present for me," she concluded. She was so pleased with the way the kids had used the time that she said, "I should let the kids do the planning."

Leonard provided many consciousness-raising experiences in the classroom. He was bright and articulate but often out of touch with the other kids. In the morning when Nancy, his aide, wheeled him into the classroom, he would be completely absorbed in reading *The Hunt for Red October* and wouldn't even look up to notice where he was. Two boys wheeled him down to lunch every day, and in November he still didn't know their names.

Rosemary felt that her training in physical therapy helped her to feel "comfortable" with people with disabilities. One day on the playground, Leonard decided he wanted to go down the slide. Nancy would start him off at the top, and Rosemary would catch him at the bottom. As Rosemary and Leonard waited for his crutches to be brought around they boogied together a bit.

Rosemary's approach with Leonard was direct—open to frank discussion. This seemed to make it easier for the other children to accept him. One exchange between Leonard and Ned during a class discussion of dreams was particularly touching. Leonard told an elaborate dream: He and his father were sailing with Columbus. Pirates were coming after them—in a computer-generated ship. Leonard jumped out of the ship and saw a pond with two ducks. He thought he could hide in the duck nest. The ducks told him to drink the water.

After a couple of other children told their dreams, Ned raised his hand and directed his question at Leonard, asking very gently and musingly, "Leonard, in your dreams, can you walk?" Leonard answered in a strong, joyous voice, "Yes, I could *run!*"

Rosemary believes that kids have a "sense of fairness," and she both relies on and builds on this in trying to make her classroom a place where differences are honored and accepted.

A Lesbian and an Activist

Over the years, Rosemary has worked for a variety of political causes in her effort to "create fairness." She is an activist in her school as well, understanding her role as involving a lot more than just her own classroom. She is a leader in her union. She serves on various committees—the Diversity Committee, the Child Study Committee. She turned the class over to Nancy one day so that she could attend a meeting at which the future of the math and science specialists was being discussed. These are always vulnerable positions; she felt she had learned a lot from the specialists and wanted to be sure her point of view was represented. She was involved in a National Science Foundation grant, working on math curriculum. When she finished, she would be training other teachers in what she had learned.

Her students were aware of her efforts to work for change and to create fairness. She described how, a few years ago, the children's interest and sense of outrage over the issue of homophobia had led them to take action themselves.

> *Rosemary:* One day we were talking about hate crimes, and I said, "You know, one of the problems is teenagers, and being mean to other teenagers who are gay and lesbian." And they said, "Well, we'd never do that! That's really terrible. We have to do something. What shall we do about that?" And a little boy who was supposed to play Paul Simon [in a skit about the presidential candidates] and was supposed to wear a bow tie said, "Yeah, and I wasn't going to come to school that day for the videotaping because people said, 'If you wear a bow tie, you're gay.'" He got up in front of the class and said, "That's not right!"
>
> So they wanted—I mean I was having a little demonstration—"We'll write letters! We'll do this, we'll do that!" And so we went to the statehouse, and they wanted to talk to their state senator who—I'd been working out of his office for two years with the Gay and Lesbian Political Caucus. So I called him, and I said, "We're coming in, and this is what the kids are interested in." And sure enough, two girls had spent their weekend writing questions for their senator and one of them was, "What do you think of gay people?"

He told them he had had a more intelligent conversation with them about politics and history and government than he had had with seniors from the high school.

Here again the students were "questioning the culture." When they wanted to take action—to find out more about these issues—their teacher had the expertise and contacts to help them do that. By raising these questions and showing her students how they can act on them, she is empowering them.

After the positive experience of coming out to last year's class, Rosemary resolved that she would do this every year. She was not sure what this year's class had learned from last year's—what the "kiddy network" had transmitted. She thought carefully about how she would tell her class. "I don't think it's wise to do it right at the beginning of the school year. They need to know me—I don't want to scare them. I mean, who knows what stereotypes they have?" She wanted to meet all the parents first at report card conferences in the fall. Then she waited for a change in the school board. A very conservative member was about to retire.

Rosemary looked for a way to begin this discussion. One morning she brought in a newspaper article on the passage that week of legislation to protect gay and lesbian students from discrimination in schools. This had been accomplished through the work of an alliance of high school students. The new law was an amendment to the same law Rosemary had worked on years before that would protect students from discrimination based on gender, race, religion, and nationality. Rosemary told me in the morning she had an idea how she could connect this with the current reading assignment in the *BFG*, one of the books by Roald Dahl. The initials stand for Big Friendly Giant. She read some of the assigned chapter aloud—ending with the part where Sophie understands that the voracious giants are heading for England. Sophie says, "We can't just do *nothing!*" Rosemary told the class she wanted to show them how some other kids saw a problem and decided they had to do something about it. She took out the *New York Times* and showed them a front-page article about the group of high school students who worked on the law to protect gay and lesbian students in school. The students organized it and went to their legislators and told them their stories. Finally the bill passed. "It was the kids who did it," Rosemary emphasized.

That was the first lesson, an empowering, activist lesson. She used this successful action of a group of high school students to illustrate what can result from that impulse of Sophie's, "We can't just do *nothing!*" She underscored her point by reminding the class that it was action on the part of kids that had changed the former racist logo for the Massachusetts Turnpike by removing the arrow through the Pilgrim's hat.

The second lesson was about discrimination. Rosemary asked the class how gay and lesbian students might be discriminated against.

> *Danny:* They might get teased.
> *Matt:* They might be discriminated against in sports—not allowed on teams.
> *Lydia:* I've been teased. Some boys in another class call me a bio-sexual.
> [Rosemary says, "You should come talk to me."]

Two other kids spoke about Black students and the discrimination they suffer. Rosemary talked about prejudice and friends and the need for kids to feel safe at school in order to study and learn. She mentioned how these issues can be worse in middle school, where these kids will be next year. Later in the discussion, Heather made the previously quoted comment, "There's a rumor that Mr. Morse is gay. Everyone is saying that." Rosemary was not prepared for this tangent! She ended the discussion by bringing it back to the *BFG*. Then the school day was over.

The bus kids left. The others were pleasantly raucous, with what seemed to me a sense of relief and release. Heather and Tina got inside a collapsible tepee that someone had brought in for the Indian unit. Henry put his face to the opening in the side and called them *weirdos*. The girls claimed he called them *lesbians* and went to complain loudly to Rosemary—so that everyone in the classroom could hear. They seemed to be working on making a connection with the earlier discussion.

When all the children had gone, Rosemary said, "Well, that was interesting!" She had been looking for a way to come out herself—not to out someone else. She said she felt Nancy's disapproval during the discussion. She wasn't out to her yet, although she figured, because they had mutual friends, Nancy must know. As she spoke of her hesitation, Rosemary was banging a ruler or something against the desk. "So I mean she can't *not* know it, but I have not sat down and said a word with her. I mean, I keep having a free period and saying, 'Now I'm going to do it,' but there's something that says to me, 'Not yet.'"

Rosemary wondered why the kids didn't ask her. She thought they must know from last year's kids. I wondered if they had forgotten or repressed this information. I had been watching and didn't see any expressions of knowing being passed back and forth among them. When she finally did tell them later in the year, she said, "No reaction. I mean like, *So?*"

Another connection that Rosemary made between her lesbianism and teaching involved the relationship she saw between homophobia and sexism. The fear of lesbianism—or of being branded a lesbian—is used to keep women in their place, to keep them from being strong and outspoken. The stereotype of the lesbian is used to enforce traditional stereotypes of women. This fear of being seen as straying outside the bounds of femininity is used to maintain those debilitating qualities of passivity, deference, and indecision. Of course, the same is also true of the way the fear of being seen as gay can influence men to be more aggressive and insensitive. Sexism and homophobia, as Rosemary emphasizes, feed on each other and must be fought together.

Collaborating and Empowering

In Rosemary's professional life there were important links between the value she placed on collaboration and her own use of power. These links could be seen in both her relationships with her colleagues and her relationships with her kids.

Rosemary thought highly of her colleagues and always spoke of them with respect and appreciation. She saw them as sharing important values of her own. As she said, "People at my school *get it* that you start teaching people to care for each other as soon as you get them in your class—you don't wait till they're fourteen or fifteen."

Unlike Lucy and Marcia, who ate lunch in their rooms, if they ate at all, Rosemary spent every lunch hour or fraction thereof with the other teachers. She made a point of introducing me to everyone. The lunch conversation involved a lot of laughter, teasing, and references to shared experiences. There was some discussion of the kids. For a couple of days, there was speculation as to whether Betsy, a student of Rosemary's, was anorexic. Betsy's friends kept reporting on what she was or was not eating at lunch. The other teachers had opinions and advice; the nurse held some discussions with Betsy and her friends; and the matter seemed to be resolved.

In that teachers' room I never heard any dumping on kids or badmouthing of colleagues, even though these are sometimes the staple of teachers' room conversation. After school on Friday, Rosemary occasionally had a beer with a group of colleagues, an event they referred to as their "stress management workshop."

My impression of Rosemary's school beyond her own classroom substantiated the positive description she always gave. It seemed to be a collaborative, supportive, friendly place. Many adults were in and out of her room—asking for help, giving help, or taking over. There seemed to be an easy, noncompetitive relationship among them, a sense of "we're in this together." I saw many examples of how Rosemary relied on this collaborative spirit to deal with problems. There was the question of Betsy and anorexia. When Lydia was called a "bio-sexual," Rosemary talked with the teacher whose student had called her that, and then *that* teacher dealt with the problem in her class. Leonard's aide took over the class when Rosemary was out of the room and at other times. The reading teacher, who was officially assigned to three children, would often develop lessons for the whole class, which would help her assigned kids without removing them or singling them out in class.

Once when an intern, who was in the class one day a week, was doing a lesson on the *BFG*, Rosemary commented to me that she would have done the lesson differently—and though this was not said in a critical manner, it indicated how collaboration like this sometimes means giving up one's own way of doing things. On another occasion, the reading teacher was in the room doing a lesson with the whole class. Rosemary gave some directions that contradicted those of the reading teacher, which the kids quickly pointed out. Rosemary said lightly, "Oh-oh, too many cooks! I'm out of here," and went off to do some xeroxing. In these examples, Rosemary shared her authority with other adults readily.

Rosemary helped other teachers, too. She often brought another fifth grade class back from lunch in order to give their teacher a few extra moments to have a smoke in her car. Sometimes she would let Mike visit her class for part of a day. He was a child with fetal alcohol syndrome who was in a special education classroom. He was assigned to Rosemary's class for "specials" like art and gym, but he came for additional visits as a reward for good behavior, and, according to Rosemary, he always behaved well while he was in her class.

Rosemary called her school "a school of aunts," which reminded me of Lucy's teacher-aunts, whom I always imagined as a sort of cloud of witnesses and supporters to her practice. Rosemary told me a story about how the teachers in her school were rallying around to help a young colleague. This teacher had taken as foster children two kids at the school who came from a large, seriously dysfunctional family. Subsequently she had adopted the children, which meant losing the foster child payments. Then her car had broken down, and the teachers were organizing transportation for her. Rosemary was very proud of the "auntly" behavior on the part of her colleagues.

This modeling of collaborative behavior in the school at large may have had an influence on Rosemary's classroom. In any case, she made a point of sharing authority with her students and encouraging them to speak for themselves.

On one occasion Ralph claimed, "Ms. Trowbridge is being unconstitutional!" He felt the strength of the rule of law behind him as he jokingly pitted that strength against her. Rosemary maintained an easy, joking relationship with the kids. One morning when I caught up with the stalled line of her class on their way out to recess, it took a while to see what was holding them up: Rosemary was scolding them for their behavior. Her tone was so light that she seemed only to be joking, but the kids did not misunderstand her meaning. They were quiet, listening.

On another morning the students were filling out cards for their "pleasure reading," on which they were supposed to spend half an hour a day at home. Rosemary reminded them of how long it had been since the beginning of the quarter and applied a little pressure. She sounded annoyed with some kids who hadn't been doing the reading or recording it. Apparently it was one of those moments of truth—they were supposed to have been keeping up with this on their own. The kids went up to her desk one by one, and she checked their cards. She questioned the accuracy of some records. Some cards weren't made out right. She was irritated, but the kids took it in stride. At the end Rosemary asked, "Have I talked to everyone? Is there anyone I haven't talked to—or yelled at—yet?"

In general, she talked to them almost as equals—the fact that several of her fifth graders were as tall as she was seemed emblematic of this relationship. She mentioned her rapport with them when I asked about discipline. "I think my classes are always well behaved. I develop such rapport with them. Sometimes we kid each other; sometimes we have to get down to work, but it's never me against them." As she spoke, she illustrated the "me against them" by knocking her two fists against each other.

One afternoon during the Indian unit, Rosemary was brainstorming project ideas with the kids and writing them on the chalkboard. She had trouble spelling *architecture* and hesitated over *diorama*. Tad—on his own initiative—looked them up in a dictionary, then came forward with a great flourish to correct the misspelled words on the chalkboard. The kids loved it. Rosemary was amused, unthreatened, and even glad that he was able to see the mistakes and correct them.

Rosemary does not present herself as a perfect teacher, but is open about her foibles. One day she temporarily lost a set of the kids' papers. "I collected your papers so *I* could lose them instead of you," she joked. While I was there she forgot glee club, band, snack, and an announcement she was supposed to send home. The assistant principal stopped by once when the class was deep in math to ask why they had not showed up at lunch yet. The kids sometimes made up for her shortcomings—they would remind her about band, find the papers, correct the spelling words, which also had the effect of empowering them.

One of the girls in the class, Lydia, who struck me as very bright and insightful, was a particular concern to Rosemary. The girl's family was going through a difficult time. She was frequently late to school. She was found by the school nurse to have scabies. She looked neglected—her clothes were too small, her hair was unkempt. Rosemary asked the school nurse to come and speak to the whole class about hygiene. She followed this up with several conversations with Lydia. I heard her say privately to Lydia, "I want you to take care of yourself. No excuses." This approach emphasized Lydia's strengths and pointed toward action she could take—

her agency in the matter—as well as assuring her of Rosemary's interest and support.

In a phone conversation a year later, Rosemary caught me up on some of her kids, now in the middle school. Lydia, she reported, had had a run-in with a substitute teacher who had said something about a student that Lydia thought was a racist remark. Lydia complained to the principal, who spoke to the sub, who was furious because one of the kids had "squealed" on her. The story reminded me of the group of girls in Rosemary's class who had complained that the sub had favored the boys. Lydia (who had probably been one of that group) had received her training in protest in Rosemary's fifth grade.

Rosemary used the curriculum to emphasize collaborative values within the class. The students enjoyed a math game that involved multiplication and strategy, which I observed. The game was played by two teams. The players on each team could ask for help from their teammates when it was their turn—but they had to ask; help could not be volunteered. This seemed a fine rule because it gave the players time to think for themselves while knowing that help was available. There was much consulting, and the kids were patient while the opposite team consulted. Some kids seemed central to the play—Ralph on one side, Ned, Lydia, and Heather on the other. Some were more apt to act on their own, others to ask for help. When it was Leonard's turn, his whole team gathered around his wheelchair. The end game got harder and the tension increased. All the Blues were concentrating and plotting. The Reds announced that they had won before I could even see it, but the Blues saw it and couldn't block them. During the game there had been no groans or put-downs as reactions to players' moves.

Toward the end of the school year, Rosemary asked me to come in specifically to see the kids work on a math project called Quilt Squares. The kids were doing a worksheet that had a grid that was made out of a series of dots. Their assignment was to divide each square on the grid as many different ways as they could think of, as long as they were divided into four equal parts. Then they colored the parts with four different colors, which they could choose, in order to make a quilt square. What Rosemary liked about this approach, she had told me earlier, was that there were so many different ways to do it, and they were all okay, as long as the four colors were equal. It seemed great for teaching fractions and also for use as a geometry exercise. The kids had to divide squares in fourths and eighths to make some of their designs.

Rosemary had started to explain how a right triangle equals half a square, when she got called somewhere else, so Matt showed Laurie. Later Laurie used this new information to explain another design to the whole class with the overhead projector. Lydia, using the overhead, showed how she made her design and why she did it that way. She was showing Henry, who had said he didn't get it. This work showed clearly who did or didn't "get it."

The project was fun to watch—diverse, as Rosemary pointed out, and collaborative. It connected art and math, which in school at least are apt to be taught separately and often viewed as distinctly female and male pursuits, respectively. It paid attention to a traditional women's art form not usually considered part of the curriculum and not something boys would do. The way the kids worked together reminded me of Rosemary talking about practicing games at recess and giving kids some experience in "being the coach instead of the star." They all became experts on their own quilt designs.

That lesson seemed to combine many elements of feminist teaching. On another occasion, when I asked which students Rosemary saw as feminists or future feminists, she mentioned Heather, Robin,—and Tad! She was thinking of children whom she saw as sensitive about issues like sexism and also able to stand up for themselves, qualities she feels are important to foster. But, she went on, "I'm hoping—I guess I'm hoping a good number of them will feel that they have enough self-esteem to speak up for themselves. I hope they all do."

NOTES

1. The "Monday morning pronoun" refers to a practice of some gays and lesbians who are not out in their workplace. On Monday mornings, when they get the typical questions about how they spent the weekend, they switch the gender of the pronoun referring to their date or partner when they talk about what they did, thus preserving an appearance of heterosexuality.

2. Postman and Weingartner (1969), Kohl (1969), Neal (1960), Cullum (1967), respectively.

3. Both of the Dahl novels that the class read while I was there, *BFG* and *Matilda* have female protagonists—certainly a mark in their favor. However, they are both profoundly sexist. For instance, in *BFG*, the boys and girls have stereotypical dreams. In *Matilda* the two teachers set up a stereotypical dualism of women's—and teachers'—roles. Worse, I suspect the name Trunchbull is a not very subtle allusion to "bull dyke."

4

Marcia:
A Sense of Community

When you learn, teach.
When you get, give.
As for me,

I shall not be moved.

—Maya Angelou

I can't call on you now.
It's a girl's turn.

—Rodrigo

My experience with Rosemary reminded me how very political teaching is. Her activism, her insistence on being out and on dealing with difficult and controversial issues in her fifth grade classroom were strong examples of this. She linked her pedagogy to her position as an out lesbian and a feminist.

The fact that teaching is political is perhaps most salient to groups of people who do not represent the "mainstream" culture, as I saw again in working with Marcia. The position of such groups gives them that "epistemological advantage." They are aware, for example, of ways in which the values of the school collide with their own cultural values. They can see how mainstream, how White, how heterosexist, and how middle class is the culture of most schools. For bell hooks in *Teaching to Transgress*, as for many African Americans and many other teachers, teaching is not merely a way of "transmitting the culture"—which implies that the culture is fine; we merely need to find more effective ways of passing it on—but of questioning, resisting, and revising that culture (hooks, 1994).

At the same time another important aspect of teaching emphasized by African American educators is its potential for "raising the race" (Collins 1991, 147). This vision of the power of education goes back at least to 1831 when Maria Stewart, in her writings and speeches, "saw the potential for Black women's activism as educators" (Collins, 4). She was followed by a number of Black women, who, as activists, teachers, writers, and founders of schools, saw education as a means of raising the race. Among these were Anna Julia Cooper, Lucy C. Laney, and Mary McLeod Bethune (Collins 1991; Giddings 1984).

Given this long-standing tradition, teaching among African American women seems linked to their sense of the historical oppression of their people and to their commitment to the community. In their book *Educated in Romance* (1990), Dorothy Holland and Margaret Eisenhart interviewed Black and White women college students about their career choices. They found Black students making clearer, more purposive career choices than White students. In my limited sample, as it happens, both Lucy and Rosemary turned to teaching in more or less accidental ways, but Marcia had *wanted* to be a teacher since she was in high school.

Another African American feminist, Patricia Hill Collins, relates the experience of Black women growing up in a racist society to the development of a certain consciousness, or awareness, a particular angle on the world. She sees experience and consciousness as interdependent. Experience contributes to the development of consciousness, and consciousness also affects how and what we experience. "African American women as a group experience a world different from that of those who are not Black and female" (Collins, 24). My experience with all three case-study teachers had reminded me of how one's own upbringing and position enable one to see some things clearly, but can also cover up, obscure, or hide essential knowledge about the world.

An example of this question of who can know what came up in a phone conversation I had with Marcia. I asked her about a summer class she was teaching about cultural diversity or, as she referred to it, teaching White teachers what they need to know in order to teach minority children. She team-taught the course with a White woman, Jane. I asked her how the class was going. She hesitated, then said, "I'm beginning to feel . . ."

"Tired?" I guessed, thinking that teaching a class right after the end of the school year would be pretty demanding.

"No . . . I'm looking for the right word, because I've been accused of not using the right words recently. I'm getting tired of teaching situations where minorities are in charge—is that putting it right?"

I didn't understand what she meant until she told me something that had just happened in class. Her fellow teacher, Jane, was away this week, so Marcia was teaching the class alone. She had a White student who kept insisting on how she had suffered from poverty and how she understood the reality of urban kids and kids of color, because she had been poor herself. In a conversation after class, Marcia said, "No, you don't understand. Now if you'd been Black, you would understand." The student started crying and accused Marcia of being a racist. Marcia tried to talk to her again later, but the student refused.

Marcia was upset in a way I hadn't heard before. She was usually pretty cool and tough, and she had certainly been there before. When her White colleague returned, Marcia said to her, "You would probably have said the same thing."

"Yes," said Jane, "and the student would have accepted it."

So this was the core of Marcia's problem of minorities in charge. It's a question of knowledge and a question of power. Marcia speaks from her "epistemological advantage." There are some things she knows from her positioning and her consciousness and her experience in the world. She understands the children she teaches in a way that a White teacher cannot. Her student, the White teacher, insists on the reality of her own suffering. She wants recognition for her poverty, her particular oppression. She also thinks that her suffering makes an *automatic* connection with poor students and students of color. Basically, as a White person, she cannot imagine that what she knows is not adequate.

Marcia denied her this easy connection. She was deeply concerned that the other teacher wouldn't get the point, that she wouldn't learn an essential message from Marcia's course, that she would go away thinking she knows all about the experience of being poor regardless of race, and that in important ways she *wouldn't* understand the kids she teaches.

Marcia felt that it was not only her knowledge but also her power that was being questioned, challenged, and resented. "It's just like when women began to get some power, be in charge of things," she said. "Men and other women resented it and thought they couldn't do it right."

During my work with Marcia I thought a lot about these questions of whose knowledge counts, who is allowed to have power, and who is denied. These are issues that White teachers face as we struggle to develop a multicultural understanding—though perhaps we don't struggle hard enough or realize how difficult it is. Lisa Delpit doesn't mince words. "[W]e must be vulnerable enough to allow our world to turn upside down," she says, "in order to allow the realities of others to edge themselves into our consciousness" (1995, 47).

Initially I had wondered if I would be able to find a teacher of color who would be willing to participate in my project. I had asked teachers at the outset if they were *feminists* and let that be a decisive criterion. I saw the term itself as problematic. Some women of color see *feminist* as a term implying White women with undertones of racism. Since my original contacts included no women of color, I asked people directly if they knew any women of color who were feminist teachers. One or two people said, "Well, let me think about it. I'll get back to you." They seemed hesitant, perhaps wondering about the label, perhaps concerned about exposing their friends to a White researcher. Finally, a friend mentioned two teachers of color with whom she worked. The first of these teachers kept putting off our interview until I realized that she really didn't want to do it. Before I called the second teacher, who was Marcia, I asked my friend to speak with her beforehand. Later when I called, Marcia said yes to a first interview.

I began my work with Marcia concerned about how she would accept me, a White feminist, as an observer in her classroom. As I started listening to her life story I was haunted by a fear similar to that recounted by Kathleen Casey in her book, *I Answer with My Life* (1993), which is based on oral history interviews with women teachers. She writes, "[T]hroughout my study of black women teachers I have been troubled by the fear that I would not be told or could not understand the life stories of this group because I am white" (1994, 107). Casey has an adopted child who is Black. She saw this as an important point of connection with the Black teachers she interviewed. I was aware that the fact that I have lesbian daughters helped me to win Rosemary's trust. I did not have such a link in Marcia's case. But the links we did have were important ones. We were both feminists, although the meaning of that might vary, and both longtime teachers of elementary school kids.

And we bonded over blood pressure. We discussed symptoms and medications and theories. Once at lunchtime I walked with her five times around an empty lot near the school. She was trying to do this regularly because of her high blood pressure. Mine has been high for years; hers had gone up recently and suddenly. Marcia saw her blood pressure as related to her personality, a kind of bodily metaphor. When I asked her about a teacher whose angry voice could occasionally be heard in Marcia's room, I was thinking how it would irritate me if I taught in Marcia's room, but Marcia's response was, "See, I wish I could be that way. She gets angry and expresses it. I don't—that's why I have high blood pressure."

Over the weeks, she let me in on many aspects of her teaching life. I went on a field trip with her class, joined a meeting with other teachers, and sat in on a parent conference with a student and her mother. Besides the after-school interviews, Marcia and I sometimes talked at lunch— although lunch was an iffy affair with Marcia. No chance of a falafel place or even a teachers' lunchroom. Sometimes she ate standing up; sometimes she bought a school lunch, then put it away until after school; sometimes she went home, which was just up the street, for the break.

Marcia had a student teacher in her room most of the time when I was visiting, and she herself left the room from time to time on various errands. On my second classroom visit, as Marcia was on her way out the door, she looked around and saw that I was the only adult left in the classroom. I felt drawn into her world when she said airily, "You're completely in charge! I do this to my friends all the time."

MARCIA'S STORY

During the spring, as Marcia and I made plans for my visits to her classroom, she mentioned a family reunion, an important biennial event on her calendar. She showed me a picture—a panoramic view that stretched across the top of two facing pages in the *New York Times*. It had been a small reunion, she said, only about 250 people were there. Sometimes 500 attend. This expanded family seems an apt symbol of Marcia's sense of connection to many people: her relatives who live at a distance, her immediate family, and the community in which she now lives and works. Marcia calls herself "a home person." A sense of family and community is an important underlying value in her life.

Marcia was born in a small town in the South where both of her parents were employed in a citrus packinghouse. Her father worked year round, making and repairing crates. Her mother worked during the citrus season, from October to April. The three children, Marcia and a younger sister and brother, stayed at home with a baby-sitter until they started school.

An illustration of what I feared, that I would misunderstand or misinterpret Marcia, occurred in an early conversation. She told how, when she was little, she and her siblings would sometimes go to work with their parents. Her story is interspersed with my comments in brackets.

> *Marcia:* And when it was time for us to go to school—we'd leave school and go where they worked. [You put in a long day.] We used to pack food. We'd take naps, get up, and work. [Your little after-school program.] We'd earn money because we could make boxes. [Even when you were little!] Yeah, it was funny because we used to—the packinghouse is completely closed now, but I used to go visit, and the people that would work—they'd be amazed. I'd come in and make boxes, and they'd look at me, "You know how to do this?" Yeah, I made boxes.
> *Carla:* Did you enjoy that?
> *Marcia:* Oh, yeah!

My comments, interwoven with this story, indicate my changing understanding of what Marcia was telling me—first seeing it as a situation calling for sympathy for the little children having to go to work with their parents; then seeing what the family made of this situation and reconceptualizing it as some kind of after-school program; finally recognizing the pleasure and sense of accomplishment Marcia remembers from those times. Marcia's tone—this was clearly a happy memory—helped me to get on her wavelength and see this situation more as she did. After all, it could be empowering for a child to work alongside her parents, to be able to make things and earn money.

Marcia describes herself at this period as "Oh, very conscientious. Always felt that I had to do well, extra well." She was the oldest child. "As my sister says, I always did everything right, and they did everything wrong." She went on, "She has always reminded me of that, because I always was the ideal person, did everything right, never . . . I mean literally, I remember when we were growing up, I used to cry because she and my brother would get spankings for doing things wrong, and I used to cry for them."

The only time Marcia recalled getting into trouble herself was also the result of her conscientiousness. In telling the following story, Marcia sometimes gives statements a questioning intonation, as Lucy did, so I use a question mark to indicate that.

> *Marcia:* No, the only thing I ever got in trouble about was—I was always— if I wanted something I wouldn't ask for it? I'd cry. So that's the only thing— like one day I wanted to go to like a Valentine party, and I needed a dollar or something, and I wouldn't ask my parents. I developed this awful stomachache. So then I cried, and they went and got medicine for me to take, and I still was crying. Then they finally went, "Now what's wrong?" I needed a dollar. So then I got a spanking *and* a dollar! Because they wanted me to start saying that I wanted things and not cry, but just ask for what I want, because they were going to give it to me. But they thought that I had lied because I'd said—My stomach *was* hurting! [laughing]
>
> *Carla:* Yeah, anxiety maybe.
>
> *Marcia:* But see, during that time, they didn't understand that. They just knew that I didn't tell them exactly what was wrong, so they figured, Let's spank her.

I assumed from her telling of this story that she was *afraid* to ask for the money, but Marcia said, "Well, not afraid, but I just felt that we didn't have a lot of money, and if something cost money, I was like, I don't know if I should ask for this or not. And then the other thing, we were given an allowance and we were told, 'You spend your allowance, and then you have no more money.'"

Here Marcia corrects my interpretation. She wasn't merely afraid; it was more complicated than that. She had some degree of understanding of her family's situation, and she felt she should have saved her own allowance.

Her memory calls up a more mature and insightful child than I was assuming, and certainly a very conscientious one. This story also shows a child who was not protected from or kept in ignorance of her family's financial situation, as many middle-class children are. Like Rosemary, thinking back on her mother's situation in life, Marcia now has a perspective on her parents that she could not have had then; she says about her anxiety-induced stomachache, "During that time, they didn't understand that."

In the schools that Marcia attended from elementary to high school during the 1940s and 1950s all the students and the teachers were African American. In her class growing up—as well as in her extended family—there happened to be many more boys than girls.

> *Marcia:* See, and that's because I grew up with all those boys. And then when my dad just—we always thought my dad wanted his first child to be a boy. So I had an opportunity to do all those things with my dad—like we did a *lot* of things. He'd take me to every football game, any baseball game, any game. I remember seeing Larry Doby.[1] He tells me I don't remember. I say, "I remember, I was on Jimmy's shoulder." I think they said I was near four. I remember they put me on Jimmy's [a friend of the family] shoulder, because they didn't want people to step on me in the crowd. I remember them saying that, "We're going to put you up so people won't step on you." So I know I had to be small, but I remember.
>
> *Carla:* So it was a privilege—to be treated like a boy?

To my mind, Marcia's statement suggests that she was "being treated like a boy" by her father. She responds in what follows, by saying that's not how she saw it. This happened several times in our conversations: I make a guess, an assumption, an inference; Marcia revises or corrects it. Again, I see my tendency to put out so many guesses as related to my fear, as Casey puts it, "that I would not be told or could not understand" Marcia's story (1993, 107), and I was glad she *would* set me straight. In this case, however, Marcia does seem to agree with me later on.

> *Marcia:* Well, I don't know if I ever thought of it [as] being treated like a boy, but just being able to do all these fun things with my dad.
>
> *Carla:* No, well, maybe you didn't think about it, but it seems like it was.
>
> *Marcia:* Yeah, because I could do all these fun things that a lot of my friends didn't get a chance to do. It was really—
>
> *Carla:* More than your sister and brother?
>
> *Marcia:* Yeah, well my sister. Now I'm trying to think why my brother didn't do a lot. I can't remember my dad ever really doing stuff with my brother like he did with me. And then, too, I think he was working more when my brother was born than with me. Because I remember he used to drive trucks for the company, and he'd take me with him, but when my brother was born, I can't remember him driving.

Marcia recollects happy memories of being included by her father when he went to sports events and to work. Her recollections point out what different experiences siblings can have, depending, among other things, on their parents' situation at the time. She thinks the fact that her father was working more and doing different jobs when her brother was little contributed to the difference she recognizes in their relationships with their father as children. Her interest in and knowledge of sports, which began at an early age, continues today and is a connection to the male world. She's proud of this knowledge and enjoys impressing and even surprising people with it.

At the time, although she acknowledges that she did "all these fun things that a lot of my friends didn't get a chance to do," she did not frame this in terms of gender discrimination, unlike Lucy and Rosemary, who both remember things they weren't supposed to do because they were girls.

> *Marcia:* So I just always had this, well, I grew up to be a tomboy. I really didn't have things girls just didn't do, but, you know, I did them because that's what I grew up doing. So I didn't change.

This statement touches on a central tenet of Marcia's feminism—the strongly held belief that girls can do anything they want to do. She bases her feminist ideas on the strength and agency of women rather than on women's oppression. Significantly, in connection with the idea of capability and in contrast to Rosemary, Marcia *was* able to use her father's tools:

> *Marcia:* That's another thing I think happens when you grow up in the environment I grew [up in], where I knew what tools were. My dad had tools, and I'd watch him, and then, I mean, there was nothing for me if something was broken—get the screwdriver, fix it back. And my mom would do things like that too. She wouldn't wait around for my dad to fix things. If something was broken, she'd fix it.

This sense of her own capability strengthens Marcia's emphasis on agency and self-reliance. A suggestion by a friend that, in order to get a better price on a new car, she should take a male friend with her infuriated Marcia. She banged a ruler on the desk as she recalled it. Her approach was to educate *herself* about cars before she purchased one. She bought a book on automotive repair so that she knew how her car functioned and even had occasion to correct the repairperson, which she enjoyed immensely.

In the following passage, while talking about her family, Marcia uses the same phrase with the identical emphasis that Lucy used in talking about her family and about why she saw her own early vision of a careerless marriage as discrepant. Lucy had said, "I came from a family in

which the women *did* things, even, I mean it was, they were teachers."
Here is Marcia's version:

> *Marcia:* Because I grew up in a house where you just *did* things, you know. You didn't really wait around for anybody to do anything for you. You made decisions. You were as great as anyone else. You could do anything.

Both Lucy and Marcia recollected this impression of women who *did* things. The sense that "you could do anything," however, is contradicted to some extent by the fact that the goals of both women, though very different, were nevertheless stereotypical female goals. As young women, the ability of all three case-study teachers to imagine a future was severely constrained by both conscious and unconscious ideas of what was appropriate for a woman.

Marcia, at first, thought she wanted to be a nurse, then later a teacher. She joined the Future Teachers of America, and an episode in her senior year of high school solidified her career decision.

> *Marcia:* My senior year they had an epidemic that put all the teachers at home, so we, we had a Future Teachers of America club? So they took all the seniors that were members of the FTA, put us on the bus, and took us to the elementary school, to work! To take care of those little kids! And we got paid, we got paid! My mom was complaining, because she was sending me to school to learn, and I was getting paid. So we took care of these little kids, and so then I decided I wanted to teach.

Marcia felt strongly supported by her parents in her desire to go to college and to become a teacher. She mentions how her mother saw this in terms of opportunities she had never had.

> *Marcia:* Yes, oh yes. Because at one point there were the three of us in school, and funds were really low at home, and I'd think, well, I'll drop out for a year until, you know, so that they could send the other two. And my mom said, "I never got a chance to go to school. I want you to go!"

Marcia went to a small, historically Black college, which provided a supportive, family-like atmosphere.

> *Marcia:* Yes, very small—800 students. A couple of the alumni would take me home to dinner every Sunday. I'd go to church with them, and we'd go home for dinner! So I never had to worry about the horrible food on campus on Sunday.

Despite the supportive atmosphere, it was at the college that, for the first time, she felt discriminated against in her studies because she was female. In high school, she said, her high school teachers "never made a distinction" between boys' and girls' interests or abilities. This was not true at her college.

> *Marcia:* Oh, when I was in college I used to really want to be, I really wanted to be like, a scientist, not a scientist as such but teach science? But then the head of the science department really had this thing that girls weren't supposed to be in science, and he let us know that he just loved to fail girls. He was, he was awful! And it was funny because two of the girls I know [who] majored in biology are both doctors now.

This academic sexism, of course, is not merely a distortion of that time and place but is still widespread. Marcia felt vulnerable, both academically and sexually, in relation to her instructors. She describes her first experience of sexual harassment:

> *Marcia:* I had lots of White instructors.
> *Carla:* And this guy, the head of the science department, was White?
> *Marcia:* Black, he was Black. Well, you know, I don't think a White instructor would have said that. It was different, and it was funny because I used to really like my White instructors better than I did my Black, because a lot of the Black instructors were very social. You know they were very, I'll never forget my social studies instructor decided that I should go out with him if I wanted an A in his class. And I wouldn't go out with him, so I got a B.

Actually Marcia did not call this sexual harassment, and she seems to treat it rather lightly here. This is another example of how she does not emphasize women's oppression in her view of the situation of women, but rather looks to women's ability and strength. She presents it as a choice on her part—she chose the B.

In the summers, Marcia was placed with a White family who lived in a northern city, by a baby-sitting program organized by her college. In this situation, she stepped into another traditional female role, in particular a traditional Black women's role: caring for a White woman's children (Casey 1993). Moreover, this role was institutionalized by a college program, which thereby seemed to grant legitimacy to this race and class distinction. Nevertheless, the job did open up opportunities for her by sending her north and exposing her to a wider world.

> *Marcia:* Fun, it was fun. It was in [city], and it is just a city that—I was over there recently—and it was just so great to see how people get along so well over there. And it was the same way when I was there. You know, you see Black and White people, Asian people all walking down the street, talking to each other.

She contrasts this openness with the greater segregation she experiences where she lives now. At the time, her experience working in a northern city provided another possible direction for her life after she finished college. She moved north.

> *Marcia:* So when I graduated I didn't want to go back to my little town. My mom didn't want me to come back to my little town, so I lived with a girlfriend here, and I worked at Liberty Mutual Insurance Company.

Marcia's mother again supports her in seeking wider opportunities than her own little town could provide. The move north stretches, but does not seem to lessen, Marcia's commitment to her family. She talks of them frequently and visits them often. She stays connected to her roots, and feels both a sense of responsibility and a deep appreciation for her "home folks."

The reason Marcia took a job at Liberty Mutual and not a teaching position is that in her last year in college, her determination to become a teacher began to waver as a result of a negative student-teaching experience.

> *Marcia:* Well, I did have doubt when I finished college, because I had a horrible student teaching. Oh, gosh was that awful. I was sick at the beginning of the semester. I had a sixth grade class—oh, were they bad—but my cooperating teacher was wonderful. She was so nice, but that's what helped me through that stage, but the kids were awful! So when I graduated, *never would I teach!* No way am I going to look at another classroom!

"Never would I teach" recalls Lucy's "I never dreamed I'd be a teacher" and Rosemary's "Why would anyone want to teach?" Marcia had been looking forward to teaching for years, but she too goes through a period of negativity, even revulsion against the idea of teaching.

The insurance company, however, turned out to be "so boring—it was *bor-ing.*" In addition, her friends reminded her of her original goals.

> *Marcia:* It was interesting because I had lots of friends that I'd made because I worked during the summers. So I had lots of friends and they all were like, "But you went to school all those years to be a teacher!"

Then she made a minor clerical error in her work at the insurance company—due, she thinks now, to her own boredom. She felt that the company had overreacted to this mistake. So after three months, she quit.

> *Marcia:* I thought, well, I'll go down and apply for a social work job because I know it was on River Street. On my way to River Street, I passed 15

Main Street, which is the place you sign up for teaching. So I thought, Well, I'll go in there. I went in—I think maybe on a Monday or Tuesday—and I got a job like Thursday.

Marcia had the goal of teaching in her mind for a long time, but she presents her final move into teaching as reluctant and accidental—not unlike the experience of Lucy and Rosemary.

This first job offer was in a boys' school—teaching a class of thirty-six boys.

> *Marcia:* I couldn't decide whether I was going to take it or not. I was really friendly with a lot of the cabdrivers, and one of the cabdrivers that night, he took me by the school, and I went, "That building, *that* building! I'm gonna work in that building, oh!" [laughing] The poor guy didn't earn any money that night. He spent the whole night talking to me about why I should teach and how my parents had sent me to school. He went through this whole thing, and the next day—it might have been the next day I was supposed to go to work. So I did. I went that day. And then another friend who'd decided, well, I've really got to teach—and since it was so far away—I was living in the Westside—they were going to drive me. He'd drive me every morning.

Marcia had a lot of support in her community for taking the teaching job. Her friends urged her to do it, reminding her of her original goals and her years in college. She also found professional support in her new position.

> *Marcia:* But I had a wonderful year, because there was another teacher, Darlene, it was her first year. I had the first grade; she had the second grade. And we had what they don't have now, we had a master teacher who actually worked with me half the day and worked with Darlene half the day.

This immediate, on-site, yearlong support is all too rare. In Marcia's case it made up for her terrible experience with student teaching and gave her a new, positive start. Support like this might also have been helpful to Lucy or Rosemary as beginning teachers, and I certainly could have used it myself.

One episode from that first year was apparently an important one for Marcia. She spoke about it in an interview and then, during a later visit, related the same story to a student teacher who had just spent a tough day (sometimes audibly so) on her own in the classroom next door. The student teacher came in at the end of the day to talk with Marcia. This version of the story is from the interview.

> *Marcia:* It was wonderful! Because she was there [the master teacher]. We had a problem, she was there to do the discipline. I'll never forget, all the kids walked to neighborhood schools. So I had a little boy, oh, he was awful, that

little guy. And the policy was, keep them after school. So I'd keep him after school, but when they'd start crying, I'd start crying, and she would sit with them while I'd go to the ladies room, so I could stop crying, [laughing] and then I'd come and sit with them.

This story recalls Marcia crying for her brother and sister when they got punished. The student teacher, when she heard this story, predicted that she would be crying that night too. "Well, you won't be the first," said Marcia in a tone both sympathetic and tough, "or the last."

Marcia taught at the boys' school for five years. During that time the principal retired, and the new principal was high-handed and interfering. An incident Marcia remembered—and told with great anger—was of a time the new principal violated her sense of family and community.

> *Marcia:* And what really got me, my grandmother died, and I had gone to Georgia, and I got back. We had lots of snowstorms, and we got those days off, or it might have been vacation, but there were some papers the principal needed that I didn't have while I was gone. And she walked in, and she never said, "I'm sorry to hear about your grandmother," but, "Where are those papers?" I thought, "This is it!" I lost eleven pounds. I was miserable. So my internist said to me, "What's the matter? You're losing all this weight. What's wrong?" And I said, "I don't know, I think it's my principal." And he said, "Well, you gotta get out of that school." So I transferred here.

The Ridley School was brand new. It was established in 1969 as an open concept school and an integrated school. In the early years, there was great enthusiasm and sense of purpose. Remembering those times, Marcia's voice is full of energy.

> *Marcia:* We were all very energetic and really eager to do new things, and it was just wonderful. You shared all these ideas, you know, you'd do a lesson and have food, and you'd invite another class. See, this wall moves, so you can get two classes together. Several teachers did team teaching. I did it for seven years. I mean we all, it was interesting, we all worked hard. We stayed here late in the evening, got here early in the morning. Then we'd go out together. It was wonderful! Then we had workshops. We worked an extra hour every day, and we got paid for that hour. And then we worked beyond that time, and we just had a wonderful time. It was really wonderful. It was nice. I was at a retirement party the other night, and somebody was saying how nice it was.

The teachers hired for the new school were more or less dedicated to open school principles. In the first years of the school, they spent three summers learning about methods and materials for this kind of teaching. Here again Marcia was in a supportive situation, where the teachers worked together to learn about teaching in an open classroom. This is a contrast to the isolation Lucy and Rosemary experienced as they struggled through their first years of teaching and tried to put new ideas into practice. In Marcia's program the teachers were required to go out to other schools in the city and give workshops for other teachers. Marcia went regularly to the school headed by the principal who had previously given her a hard time as well as to other schools.

Perhaps it is no coincidence that all three of the feminist teachers in this study had early and influential experience in open education. They all started teaching in the late 1960s and early 1970s, and open education represented the exciting, change-oriented programs of the time. Several of the "women teaching for change" whom Kathleen Weiler (1988) interviewed also worked or had worked in alternative, change-oriented programs.

During the same period the Women's Movement was gaining in strength. Both Lucy and Rosemary had experienced the movement as empowering and enlightening. Marcia felt that she already knew from her own experience and upbringing much of what the Women's Movement was "discovering." When I first asked her about her feminism, Marcia said she thought she'd always been a feminist. Later, I asked if she could think of any particular incident that had made her more conscious of her feminism. She remembered,

> *Marcia:* Maybe when, when women started with NOW and all that. Because I used to get really upset, because I thought they were making big productions over things I'd always thought, you know. It just, um, I sometimes felt that they were making things harder for women at some point, because some of us really had always felt that the sky was the limit and never really had problems, you know, with males.

Marcia does not recollect here her experience with the college professor who gave her a *B* or the one who discouraged her from science. She certainly did not make "big productions" of these events, either at the time or when she recollected them. The early Women's Movement was for the most part based on the needs and concerns of White women and held little appeal for Marcia, despite her own feminist beliefs.

Since the early days of open classrooms—and of the Women's Movement—Marcia's school has changed; it got caught up in the broader issues of integration and politics. The city schools were desegregated in 1975, and there was a need for teachers of color in schools throughout the city. As a result, many teachers were moved from the Ridley School to other schools. When the principal found that she was losing half her staff, she took the matter to court. She won, in that she was allowed to keep more of her teachers, including Marcia.

Marcia remembered that again in 1983, in another attempt to desegregate the schools, many White teachers were laid off. "That took all the teachers who had been here and trained when I trained. They all left because they were actually bounced out. They had no jobs."

These changes decimated the staff that had originally supported open classrooms so effectively and enthusiastically. Marcia's current principal, however, still supports the idea of open education and insists on one aspect of it, multiage groupings. Marcia believes, however, that the only other teacher in the school who really practices open education is Rhonda, who was Marcia's pupil, and who did her student teaching in Marcia's classroom. Now Rhonda teaches in the room next door, and together Rhonda and Marcia reenact some of the spirit of the early days of the school. They often stay at school into the evening, talking, working in their rooms, getting things together for the next school day. In the second year of my study, a young African American woman did her student teaching in Marcia's room. Like Rhonda, she had gone to the Ridley School and had been Marcia's pupil. She hoped to teach there, too, after she was certified, and a year later she was doing just that. Marcia stands as a central figure in this continuity of teachers.

Marcia's commitment to her community does not end with her long days at school. She lives in the same neighborhood. In fact her house is just around the corner from the school. In this respect, she is unlike both Rosemary and Lucy, who live in different towns from those in which they teach and therefore have less involvement with or firsthand knowledge of the particular communities that surround their schools.

Marcia has always done other work in her community as well.

> *Marcia:* Oh, yeah, I always did something else. I never just taught. Either I worked at the boys' club or at Johnson Park. These were all summer, or after-school programs I'd do, Neighborhood House, Douglas House. I've always worked someplace else—sometimes with kids, sometimes with adults, depends on the program.

Teaching elementary school is certainly a very demanding job, and Marcia puts a great deal of time and thought into it. But she "never just taught." She mentioned teaching basic education at night, where her classes sometimes included former students or even parents of her current students; supervising GED exams; taking a photography course; doing audiovisual ministry at her church; participating in innovative math programs; and teaching workshops and courses for teachers. She also appeared on a television program, talking about her teaching ideas.

Marcia taught Sunday school for years. She told me the following story about one of her former pupils.

Marcia: As a matter of fact, one's now a state trooper. I keep telling him, "You're the reason I quit teaching Sunday school!" He was one of my Sunday school kids that was so awful. And he occasionally . . . I used to be riding along, and I'll look up and see this blue light flashing behind me, and I'll go, I didn't do anything wrong. And he'd pull up, and he would find the busiest place in the city to do this stuff, so that everybody around would see him. And you know, he thought it was a big joke. And I'm like, this is embarrassing! He's probably, oh, he's about 6'5", 240 pounds, and he'd love to say, "This is my second grade teacher!" People [would] look at me [and say]—"You taught *him!*"

Besides this other work in the community, Marcia maintains contact with many of her former pupils. I've mentioned the two students who came back years later as student teachers. While I was observing Marcia's classroom, another former student came back just for a visit. One day after school Marcia was debating whether to stay and work, which is what she felt like doing, or go out in the rain to a ball game where a former student was playing. His mother had died during the past year, and he had asked Marcia to come watch him play. Of course, she went.

In her book *Black Feminist Thought* (1991), Patricia Hill Collins uses the term *othermother* to describe women like Marcia, who are so connected with the community and so important in the lives of many other people. Grandmothers, sisters, aunts, cousins, neighbors, and teachers can be part of this longstanding *othermother* tradition. According to Collins, othermothering is "both a continuation of West African cultural values and functional adaptations to race and gender oppression. . . . Children orphaned by sale or death of their parents under slavery, children conceived through rape, children of young mothers, children born into extreme poverty or to alcoholic or drug-addicted mothers, or children who for other reasons cannot remain with their bloodmothers have all been supported by othermothers" (119–20).

In her life, Marcia connects her work in school with work in the broader community, where she teaches, advises, and encourages older kids and adults. In her classroom, she emphasizes the value of community and also continually draws lines of connection between her own group of first and second graders and the community in which they live.

MARCIA'S CLASSROOM

Marcia gave me careful directions to her school. One street, like many in this city, changed its name no less than three times along the way, but she said to stick with it. This proved to be the hardest part of getting there. The Ridley School is located on a broad avenue lined with trees, which were at the time in early leaf, and a wide assortment of buildings: handsome old houses, storefronts—some of them boarded up—new buildings, a clinic, a couple of churches. On another occasion, at the beginning of the school day, the street was full of groups of children, all with adults, making their way to school. Simultaneously children were pouring out of buses. It was a busy, cheery scene.

The school itself looks rather like a fortress. As with two other urban schools I visited during this project, it was hard to locate the entrance. This is partly a matter of architectural style. Schools built in the second half of the twentieth century, rather than boasting the grand, columned entrances of earlier buildings, have more modest and practical entryways. But in many present-day schools, some of the original doorways have been changed or removed. There remain only one or two closely guarded entrances.

At the Ridley School I followed a sign that pointed to the Parents' Entrance across a wide terrace. It would be here, where a little later in the spring, a raised bed of bright flowers would suddenly be planted one Saturday by a coalition of teachers, parents, and students. I followed the sign and finally located the door, but it had no apparent doorknob or handle, and there was no response to my knock. Did I need to know a magic spell? Fortunately, a real parent came along just then and pressed a doorbell that was about six feet off the ground. I followed him in.

Once past that forbidding entrance, I entered, if not a magical, certainly a very warm and inviting world. And for me an *other* world, as it was so distinctly and exuberantly a world of color. People of color were running the show. Most of the administration, office staff, faculty, paraprofessionals, lunchroom and custodial staff, guards, and students were people of color. The posters on the walls celebrated heroes and heroines of many cultures. My experience entering this school for the first time made me realize what a profound sense of otherness many children of color must experience when they enter public schools that are predominantly White in their personnel, assumptions, and trappings.

One morning I came in just as the bus kids arrived. The line moved through the school to the playground where the children reorganized themselves into their own classroom lines. Along the route were stationed several adults who would greet each child pleasantly. They said, "Good morning!" rather than, "Hi!" Often they would ask a question or make a comment that indicated that they had some knowledge of these kids and what went on in their lives outside the classroom. They regularly reminded boys with hats to take them off. The note of mannerliness—even formality—was struck at the very beginning.

The Ridley School, which now holds 608 children, was built in 1970 as an open school. The term *open*, as in Herbert Kohl's (1969) book, *The Open Classroom*, implies a more informal relationship between teachers and students; lots of hands-on, innovative materials; a child-centered curriculum based on students' needs and interests; and a multigraded division of students.

Open can also refer to the structure of the school, to different divisions of the interior space. In the Ridley School groups of five or six classrooms surround a central area where joint activities can take place. The classes in each of these groups run the gamut from first to fifth grade (rather than having all the fifth graders together, for instance), which lends something of a sense of family. Each classroom has two grades; Marcia had first and second graders. Each pair of classrooms shares a common, movable wall that can—or at one time could—be folded back. It was apparent from the arrangement of furniture in Marcia's room that this had not happened in a long time.

The school was homier without the long corridors, but the arrangement made it easier to get lost. On my first visit, I waited in the office until Larry, with a hall pass hanging around his neck, came down to bring me to Marcia's room, and it wasn't until my *fourth* visit that I found her classroom on my own. Clearly, finding my way was an issue for me at this school.

There were twenty-six children in Marcia's class—twelve girls and fourteen boys. This is a large group for the younger grades, and the room sometimes seemed very full, although never out of control. Most of Marcia's first and second graders—whom she called her Whiz Kids and Superstars, respectively, to avoid the grade assignment—were African American children. One boy and one girl were Latino. Two boys were White. Marcia mentioned a variety of jobs that were held by her kids' parents. One worked at a printer's, another at the IRS. There were a minister, a lawyer, a prison guard, a baker, a scientist, a couple of students, housewives, and teachers. One parent worked at a children's home, and one was a nurse at a nearby hospital. Some children lived with grandparents, two in foster families, and one in a shelter for the homeless.

In what follows, I will discuss Marcia's classroom. The material from my observations and discussions with Marcia is organized into themes connecting her classroom practice, the story she told me of her life, and the ideas that are important to her. First I will detail some of the many connections Marcia made between life in school and life at home. Next, I will discuss how she handled discipline and authority, look at connections and overlaps between the ideas underlying open classrooms and feminist pedagogy, and identify some challenges presented by this classroom in providing both protection from and connection with the outside world. Finally I will pull together some of these themes in contemplating Marcia as a teacher and othermother.

School and Family

Marcia's story of her life emphasized how important her family was to her as she was growing up and still is today, though they live at a distance. Her position as a teacher seems to provide her with a second family, and her classroom seems to be a second home—both for her and for her students.

Once when Marcia and I talked just at the end of spring vacation, I was remembering out loud how difficult I used to find the transition from vacation to my teaching schedule. Marcia did not feel this way. She was eager for school to begin again. Most days she gets to school early, and often, after the children have left, she spends the rest of the afternoon and early evening in her room, "getting things ready for my little children." She has a telephone in her classroom,[2] an unusual feature and one that adds to the sense that this is her place. She seems to spend more time here than at her own house, which is just a few blocks away.

Marcia has been at the same school for twenty-five years, giving her experience there great depth and continuity. A first and second grade combination like hers is sometimes called a "family grouping," because the mixing of children of different ages is more like a family than having a group of same-aged children. This arrangement means that Marcia has her students for two years. Thus she knows her students well, and she knows their families—not just through school but through her church, the adult education courses she teaches, and community programs in which she participates. The power of these connections is not lost on the kids. "Lawrence," she would say, "I saw your aunt at church last night. She asked how you were doing." Lawrence would sit a little straighter and focus a little harder.

One morning Marcia brought in a section of the local newspaper that dealt with violence in the schools, which she wanted to discuss with her class. There was a story about two children, cousins, who started out "play fighting," but one ended up getting stabbed. Marcia expressed her amazement. "I love all my cousins," she said. Then Natalie talked about fighting with her sister, and several children said they fight with their sisters. Marcia asked, "Now *why* would you want to fight with your sister?" She shows a concern for the children's families and how they get along. She also seems to offer the (loving) family as a metaphor for relationships at school.

A sense of the classroom as a family was evident in the daily ritual of show-and-tell. This was an entirely kid-run operation in which Marcia usually did not interfere, although she listened carefully. Show-and-tell took place without fail first thing every morning. As soon as the children came into the classroom, they would check the class list to see whose turn

it was to run show-and-tell. That child would stand, leaning against a certain desk at the side of the room. After they had put their things away, the
other children would group themselves in a small, designated area on the
carpet nearby. The leader would begin with the ritual line, "Anyone for
show-and-tell?" This question would be asked, even if half the students
were already waving their arms eagerly. The leader then would call on
girls and boys alternately, a practice they themselves had established earlier in the year. As each child was called, he or she would stand next to the
leader and talk. Children who had something to show would usually
keep it hidden—either in their book bags or under their sweatshirts—and
pull it out at the perfect dramatic moment. After all the other children had
had their turns, the leader would take his or her turn last. What follows is
an example from my field notes for a Monday morning. The children's
comments are abbreviated.

Matt is in charge of show-and-tell.

Lawrence: My sister taught me how to iron my own pants. I saw Norton on
the monkey bars. [Marcia, who is moving around organizing things, asks
him, "What playground?" She has her ideas about which ones are safe.]
Girl: I have new sneakers.
Rodrigo: Yesterday at my grandmother's I made a new instrument [a mu-
sical instrument, which he shows]
Zoe: Yesterday I got some new clothes. Here is my T-shirt. [Marcia and I
can't hear what she says, but the other kids can, and they repeat it for us.]
Mark: Somebody came to fix the alarm at my house.
Rosita: Sunday I got this [pulls a box out from under her shirt—it holds a
ring]
Charles S.: Yesterday after school I went to karate. I saw Leroy on his bike.
Manuel: I made this today before school. [He has a drawing of a car—when
he holds it up, the kids point out that his fly is unzipped. With a grin, he zips
it up.]
Zenia: Dad brought me to school in the truck. He stopped for the paper.
[She has her book bag with her. She pulls out the paper and shows a page
about the eclipse.]
Raoul: I went to the doctor. I saw Norton at the Food Basket—something
about Nintendo.
Boy: Last night at the park I saw _____ and _____.
Raina: [pulls catalogue out from under her shirt and points] I might get this
or this.
Roland: My dad got a pencil stuck in his hand. He had to go to the hospital. [His details are a little gross. He seems overwhelmed by the effect of his
description. He goes back to his place and buries his head in his knees.]
Harriet: Yesterday I stayed home. My mother curled my hair. [Nothing is
said about the legitimacy of this excuse.]

Nathan: This morning my mom woke me up. On the radio I heard about the eclipse.

Bruce: Yesterday I went to the arcade. I played Immortal II, Something Champions. That's it. [A lot of them use this phrase to mark the end of their offering.]

Leroy: Yesterday I did my homework, something else. That's it.

Matt: Yesterday I ___. Last Friday I ___, and that's it.

Show-and-tell is finished at 9:47—it took only about twenty minutes for all this information and reconnecting.

Show-and-tell was an inclusive event. Everyone got a chance to talk, and Marcia said they all did talk during show-and-tell. Moreover, with rare exceptions, the other kids listened, or at least were respectfully quiet. The leader called alternately on girls and boys as long as this was possible. Since there were more boys, some of them had to wait till the end. This, according to Marcia, had been the students' own idea because they observed that when a boy was in charge he only called on boys.

When the kids noticed that Manuel's fly was unzipped, they didn't laugh or tease him. They merely mentioned the fact in a responsible way that seemed to suggest their concern for him and their sense that this was information he would want to have. In their talk, four children—Leroy, Charles J., Rene, and another boy—mention classmates they saw *outside* of school—on their bikes, at the Food Basket, in the park. Although in this example it is only the boys who mention seeing each other, at other times girls do this too. Their mention of these sightings seemed to me to extend the family metaphor outward. It isn't just in school that they relate to each other, and even a glimpse in another setting seems worth mentioning.

Marcia saw show-and-tell as a key part of the day. It gave her time to sort papers or check notes that the kids had brought in from home. And it gave the children a chance to talk and her to listen, serving a function similar to Lucy's "curtain time." Show-and-tell was very important to the kids, too. One morning their day started with a trip to the auditorium to see *Aladdin*. During the film, the children kept checking with Marcia to be sure they would still have show-and-tell when they got back to their room.

Marcia built upon the family metaphor in other ways in her classroom. Like both Lucy and Rosemary, she was very interested in math. She served on the math curriculum committee at her school and had both participated in and taught outside workshops and math courses. Her room contained a good supply of hands-on math materials. She spoke rather scornfully about the math textbook, but she enjoyed teaching math in innovative ways. Following is a lesson in which she uses the idea of family

as she introduces her first and second graders (her Whiz Kids and Superstars) to math facts.

Marcia starts by asking, "Matt, how many in your family?" She writes 5 on
the chalkboard, then shows different ways it can be divided up—males and
females, adults and children, mom and others—coming up with different addends of five. Then she illustrates these numbers in red and white interlocking blocks, stacking them up against the board, thus showing the facts of five.

She then asks questions about the "six family." There's lots of participation. The kids have their own blocks to work with. As Marcia calls on different kids, she sometimes tells the other children to put their hands down so
the one called on has enough time to think. Rene gives an answer: 2 + 2 + 2.
"Yes, for your group," Marcia responds. She is looking only for pairs of addends. Then, as if Rene's response has reminded her that this is easy for some
of them, she passes out worksheets to some of the Superstars, but she keeps
four second graders with the first graders.

Marcia continues with the kids left in the group. Two volunteers stand up
holding addends of six in two colors. Marcia asks various questions. At one
point Charles J. corrects her. "Oh, you're right," she says. She calls these
groups of numbers "families," which emphasizes the way they vary but still
belong together. In the middle of the exercise, the phone rings. The kids wait
while Marcia answers briefly.

At the end of the lesson, Marcia gets the class to pick up the blocks by putting them together in stacks of ten of the same color, which turns out to be
another exercise in addition—"I need two more yellows," and so on.

In Marcia's class, whole-group sessions like the one just described were
mixed with periods of time when there were many different things going
on—some assigned activities, some choices. Like Lucy's students, these children were used to making choices and moved easily from one activity to another. This particular afternoon ended with one of those wonderful moments in teaching when everybody seems to be pulling together and feeling
good about themselves and each other. To say this is "like a family" is certainly to idealize "family," but the feeling of connection at such a moment
does seem to go beyond the ordinary relationships found in a classroom.

The kids ease back into the room. Some pick up books or their thank-you
cards for Norman. Marcia hands out double-lined pages with the title "The
Movie Theater" at the top. This is for Nicole, whose last day is tomorrow.
Marcia sits with the children correcting, encouraging, coaxing, demanding—
"Get those capital A's out of your name, Jamaica." She copies Deshi's labori-
ously produced sentences for her to copy again (with much praise).

Marcia plans to collect three items from each student—their letters to Norman, their writings for Nicole, their pictures about the puppet show. When the
kids are done they can have popcorn. The kids are very busy. There's a lot of
talk about how do you spell ____? They read their stuff to each other and make
comments. Marcia moves the kids who are not finished and starts serving pop-

corn—a glassful scooped out of a large container and dumped onto a paper towel. There's no hurry or anxiety about the popcorn. Some kids go on to other things—a few math books, Leroy with a Dolch crossword puzzle book. They pull these materials from their cubbies. Rene is still finishing his letter.

At some point the kids start singing. Marcia puts on the tape of "We Are the World; We Are the Children," which they've been learning in music class for a concert next Saturday, and they practice lustily. The music soars; Harriet spontaneously starts to conduct; some children begin picking up the room in rhythm to the music. Everyone is singing. A real high.

Discipline and Authority

In *The Feminist Classroom* Frances Maher and Mary Kay Tetreault discuss how, through their research in other college teachers' classrooms, they were able to acknowledge and confront some of their own assumptions about feminist teaching. They found that "the ideal of a democratic and cooperative feminist teacher had been an example of our mistaking the experience and values of White middle-class women like ourselves for gendered universals" (1994, 15). I started this project with similar unconscious expectations about what feminist practice would look like. I also thought I would find "democratic and cooperative" classrooms, where authority would be muted and gentle. In each classroom I questioned my own ideas about authority against the models I saw being played out in the different classrooms. It seemed to me that Lucy strove for that democratic style. She listened to her students and gave them plenty of input into classroom procedures and curriculum. Rosemary relied on her rapport with the students and generally got their cooperation, although she occasionally threatened and scolded them. At first, I could not get a bead on Marcia's authority. It seemed invisible. Her classroom ran smoothly, at times without apparent control. The children just seemed to know what to do. They took turns, formed lines, got their work done, and cleaned up with very few reminders.

But now and then there were public disciplinary moments. Marcia would use a public voice when chastising an individual child. Instead of bending over and speaking in a low voice to Charles S., she would pick up his paper and say so all could hear, "You have to read that part first, before you do the questions. You don't read that fast." At first these moments felt uncomfortable to me. Why expose Charles S.? Gradually, I came to reinterpret this exposure. It did not cover up Charles's mistakes, but it did not lead the other kids to tease him either. And it served to remind everyone of Marcia's expectations.

Marcia would refer to herself in the third person, "Now what did Miss Roberts *say* about cutting in line?"—a distancing, teacherish way of talking that I have always disliked. She would stand at her full height and look down with warmth but also from a position that emphasized the distance between the authority and the erring child. Again in the way she phrases her question, she reminds the child of her expectations.

Cynthia Ballenger (1992), a White teacher who taught in a Haitian preschool, writes about how she had to examine her own assumptions about discipline and revise her discipline strategies with the help of Haitian friends and colleagues. Following their advice she tried strategies that emphasized connections between home and school values, tapping in to the children's knowledge of appropriate behavior, and insisting that the children know and abide by the teacher's expectations. In contrast, Ballenger found that the "North American teachers" avoided reprimands, emphasized individualistic values, and assumed that they *could* understand and interpret the child's feelings. Throughout this project, but especially in Marcia's classroom, I began to see how "North American" my own ideas about teaching, my assumptions about kids, my values, my expectations of feminist teachers were. I had to take a hard look at my own values as well as to listen closely to Marcia. Her authority, more like that of the Haitian teachers, is based on her knowledge of her students, her clear statement of her own expectations, and her position as the one who stands for and insists on school values that are common to all.

In an interview, Marcia referred critically to Dr. Spock,[3] an authority on whom I had relied heavily as a young mother. She associated his advice with the efforts of parents to listen and understand, an emphasis on talk that Marcia felt led to a tendency to let kids get away with things. Once in a math game she fined Mark for talking out of turn. It was obvious from his face that he thought it was not fair, but he handed over the payment (in fake dollars) without comment. Marcia said later that she *doubles* the fine if the kids make an objection. She doesn't want to hear their arguments. Her point is that the children need to know and respect the rules.

Lisa Delpit (1988) stresses the need for teachers of children of color and children of the poor to explicate the values of the school and not to assume that students in their classrooms understand or share their own values or the school's values. Delpit is thinking not only of success in school. There are important power issues here. The "mainstream" values of schools are for the most part those of the wider society. Children who do not have access to those values will not have a chance to participate in or to seek to change that power.

Marcia did not assume that the children knew how to behave in school or with each other. She frequently discussed manners and behavior with them. Sometimes she even gave the kids words to say, words that suggest an alternative response emphasizing respect and avoiding violence. In the discussion of the newspaper article mentioned previously, Marcia read a quote in which someone said, "You're entitled to your own opinion, but . . . " She paused and remarked, "Now that's something I'd *love* to hear—for someone in my class to say, 'You're entitled to your own opinion.'"

The discussion went on to the issue of forming lines. In most elementary schools, of course, there is a great deal of line formation and much passionate discussion of "cuts," "fronts," and "backs." Marcia asked her students, "What do I say when you tell me so-and-so cut?" The children responded in chorus with what apparently is her standard line, "We're all going to the same place."

"Does that solve the problem?" she asked. "Why do I say that? Because *it doesn't matter*, since we're all going to the same place." This exchange again sounds like Ballenger's Haitian teachers. Here Marcia, like those teachers, asks a question and gets a choral response—the same response from all, because all the kids know what *her* answer is. They might not agree so easily if she had asked for *their* ideas or feelings, but she didn't. In this exchange, she wanted to reinforce her values, the shared values of her classroom and the school.

"What if a kid is slow in line?" she asked.

Mark suggested, "Maybe he had to tie his shoe."

"What could you say?" she asked again.

"Excuse me, the line is moving," he answered.

I followed many lines through the intricate mazes of the Ridley School. A few days after this discussion, we filed down to the auditorium. The children were very quiet. They walked in an exemplary line. The first child in line held the first door they encountered, then waited for the end of the line. The next in line held the second door. This happened for about four doors. Jamaica stopped to tie her shoe, then she too waited for the end of the line.

The kids knew Marcia's expectations. On two occasions they showed that they knew how they measured up individually as well. One time was at a puppet show, where we filled four rows in the auditorium. Marcia surveyed the rows with a practiced eye and moved a few kids. She put Jamaica between two boys. "Let's see, who else do I have to move?" she asked. Bruce and Charles J. say, "Us." Marcia laughed, "Then why do you two sit together?" She moved them—it was all very good-natured.

Another instance of the kids' self-assessment occurred in the same discussion of the newspaper article mentioned earlier. Marcia read a second example from the paper: If someone shoves you, should you shove them back? This was immediately followed by a chorus of, "NO!"

"Who here does shove back?" she asked. The hands of three boys and two girls went up (including Roland and Natalie). Marcia surveyed them and nodded, "These are the right hands."

It is notable that in both instances the children are considering their *own* behavior. They don't accuse each other. Marcia went on, "What else could you do?"

Mark said, "It might just be an accident."

Natalie protested, "My mom says to hit back."

Marcia responded very diplomatically, "Now maybe she's thinking of when she was in school, but it's not OK, not now and not in school." Marcia was smiling and encouraging as she told Natalie she really wanted her to *try hard* not to push back in school. There's an interesting twist in this last example, when Natalie mentioned a discrepancy between what she is taught at home and what she is taught at school. Marcia's response was respectful of Natalie's mother. She did not refute her, and her answer to Natalie left room for the very real possibility that outside of school Natalie may at some time *need* to "hit back." But Marcia emphasized that it is different here at school now, and Natalie must learn the school's rules.

Besides the general discussions about behavior and the more public criticisms mentioned previously, Marcia also talked privately with individual kids. Occasionally, while things were chugging along in the classroom, she would say, "Roland, can I talk to you a minute?" (It was very apt to be Roland.) The question was lightly asked, and it took me a while to realize—what of course the kids already knew—that this "talking to" involved some infraction of the rules. Marcia's voice was low and intense. Roland stood very straight and still, quaking slightly in his light-up sneakers.

Another time Marcia had a "talking to" with Zoe and her sister, who was in another class. Their grandmother had called because she had found a watch at home that didn't belong to either of them. Zoe had a history of "finding" things that got lost, but she would eventually give them up. Apparently, Marcia and the grandmother stayed in close touch about these events. Zoe was one of the kids Marcia worried about.

Marcia sometimes moved kids who were not getting their work done to another place in the room. One time the children had a writing assignment about the puppet show they had seen on Friday. There was a lot of talking. Marcia reminded them, "Miss Roberts wants you to start writing." Charles J. continued talking. Marcia said, "Charles J., I want you to take your letter and go sit next to Harriet and write. Then we'll let you come back." This seemed to have a cohesive angle to it that related to the sense of community—you have to move away from the group for a while; then when you've done your work you can be a part of it again. Marcia often moved Roland too, keeping him right next to her.

Rene was another child who got a lot of "talking to" and a lot of close supervision. Once he provoked Marcia to anger by his incessant talking. "Can you stop talking for three minutes? That's all I hear. I'm losing it."

The following year, Marcia reported that Rene, who had moved on to a third and fourth combination grade, was floundering. She was still concerned about him and showed her continuing support by offering to his new teacher (in her first year) to take him back at any time. The new teacher could just send him in with his work to sit in Marcia's class. "I have a seat in my room for you," she said to Rene. It was a warm invitation with an edge of threat. Rene had come in once when he missed out on a field trip, and Marcia said he worked hard all day.

Most discipline issues were handled by talking to the child or moving him or her temporarily. And sometimes kids would lose their recess. One Monday, for reasons I didn't learn, several kids lost their recess from the previous Friday. They were supposed to be sent back to the room after lunch, but the lunch aid forgot. Marcia went after them. Later she said,

> *Marcia:* Well, I try to be very firm with them—follow through if I say I'm going to do something. Like today when I told them not to go out to recess. And I missed picking them up in the cafeteria. I just went out and got—
> *Carla:* Was that that group of kids who came in?
> *Marcia:* Mm-hmm, they weren't supposed to go out to recess. And see, I wasn't there when they sent them out, so they went out. And Miss Ridgeway was all apologetic because they usually ask the kids who's supposed to stay in, and they didn't. I said, "Miss Ridgeway, this is better. They got a little taste of running and playing and now they come back up and—"
> *Carla:* It makes the punishment worse, you mean?
> *Marcia:* I talked to them before I brought them back up—like each one had to tell me why they were coming back in. That's one thing I find that in discipline kids need. You really need to talk with them about why this is happening, so they can understand. They each could tell why, and they point out that one thing.

The children who were brought back helped Marcia sort papers and stuff homework folders, or they carried on with their own work. The mood was relaxed and friendly, but it was not recess.

Both Lucy and Rosemary had threatened the loss of recess on occasion or actually said, "OK, no recess for you!" then decided not to follow through with it. The child or children went out anyway. In some cases, the teachers figured that the point had been made, and with some kids it probably had. Marcia believed it was important to be very careful about what she threatened or promised and to be consistent in following through.

Lisa Delpit discusses the importance of this specificity in discipline; she is critical of teachers who are vague and allusive (1988). Marcia mentioned a discussion of language and discipline in the summer workshop that she and her White colleague Jane taught for teachers. The participants, mostly White, were observing "minority" teachers, as Marcia called them, teaching minority kids. The teachers sometimes used a phrase like, "Get off your butt and do it!" A couple of the workshop participants objected to this language, considering it "too strong" for children. Marcia quoted her colleague talking to the participants, "You could say to a middle-class child from [a wealthy suburb], 'Don't you think it's time for you to read a book?' And the child would go over and read it, but if you say it to one of the children in this group, they're going to look at you and say, 'No-oo.' So you say, 'Go read a book!' Lucy also mentioned changing her phraseology to be more directive with her class—saying, "Rosie, sit down" instead of "Will you please take your seat?"

Marcia is clear about her expectations, but she does not have a written list of classroom rules. In an interview she said she sometimes thinks she ought to, then she remembers the first graders who return for second grade. "Yeah, and they can tell them. That's why I don't need them written! I think that's the real advantage in multigrade, you know, you always have got these different kids who know what things they're supposed to be doing." Marcia never has a completely new class. This is another continuity in her teaching life. It's a different arrangement than that of Lucy, who has a new class every two years.

I commented once on how carefully the children, who were lining up for lunch, stepped over several piles of paper that Marcia had been sorting on the floor. "They've learned!" she said. In fact, she thought that in some cases, "Kids learn faster from other kids, at least things like the rules and classroom routines."

Open Classroom and Feminist Pedagogy Overlaps

When I first entered Marcia's classroom, with its cubbies and tables and clipboards for working on the floor and variety of materials and storage problems, it struck me like a familiar tune that I couldn't immediately place. This is how I described it:

> The kids have just come back from art. They go to their tables—all the groups but one seem to have both boys and girls. Marcia mentions a math paper that needs correcting. I don't know if this is for everyone. The kids are talking and doing different things. Then they spread out—several do a phonics game on the computers. Two boys bring math papers, clipboards, and tiles and do corrections of their math papers on the floor in front of me. Other kids are at their desks with various things. A girl goes into a corner with a recorder and music book. Later two other girls get their recorders (all in cases in a box) and join her.

I wondered, is this free time? Are they just finding things to do because school is almost over? It wasn't until Marcia mentioned her experience with open classrooms that I recognized this as an old friend, an open classroom.

Once a friend, with whom I had been talking about my interest in feminism and elementary schools, asked me what I thought a feminist elementary classroom would look like. Halfway through my description I realized that I was describing the alternative school I had recently left. Its philosophy was based on learning that is active, participatory, whole-child, hands-on, independent, self-directed, and empowering. The learning that this philosophy advocates seems to me to have overlaps with feminist education. Marcia's classroom embodied many of these principles. It offered numerous examples of students making choices, learning from each other, contributing to the curriculum, and taking responsibility for their own learning.

There were many periods of time when the kids could make choices about what they did. These times were not labeled, but they were similar to Lucy's free time, except that the choices were somewhat different. Marcia's classroom was small. There was no space for a block corner or art corner, and there weren't a lot of art supplies available. But there were many computers, which were used mostly for math and spelling games. There were lots of books, a box of recorders, and markers and crayons on every table. Despite the crowdedness of the room, the kids moved around freely, changing places, taking clipboards to work on the floor, spilling out into the hall. Sometimes Marcia or the student teacher would work with an individual or group while other children were engaged in a variety of different tasks. The following excerpts from my notes illustrate such moments:

> Mark and Bruce are working on a difficult word-find (words that have contractions) on the computer. They are doing very well. Every time they get one right, they get up and do a little dance. Raina and Nathan are doing a board game involving counting with different intervals. Two girls and two boys are individually hooked up at computers with earphones.
>
> During all this time, there has been no general announcement of what kids need to be doing. Some individuals have been reminded to finish their rewrites of the movie report or to work in their math books. Otherwise things just chug along.
>
> The Superstars finish their reading and decide to play their recorders. Harriet is in charge. She tries to get them to play one line at a time. There's a group working with the pattern blocks—Jamaica, Norton, and, later, Matt. Zenia's group is still coloring versions of the state seal of Connecticut. Charles S. has done several very neatly.
>
> Nathan and Roland are sprawled on the floor with clipboards, working on their weather charts. They are totally undisturbed as Deshi, on her way to the homework box, steps right over their work. There are three somewhat older boys who are camped out here for the day. Their class went on a field trip, and, for reasons unknown to me, they were left behind, bringing their work to this room. In this setting they present a contrast, fooling around, checking to see if Marcia is watching, making a great show of working if she glances in their direction.

These three visiting boys served to highlight how involved and self-directed Marcia's kids were. None of her children paid much attention to them, much less imitated their behavior, but went on about their business, which, as this sample shows, could range anywhere from computer games and musical instruments to math manipulatives, writing, and art projects.

Marcia had said how she believes kids learn from each other, and she encouraged her kids to do this. One day when she and I were watching a videotape of her class, Marcia noticed Charles J. helping Charles S. She liked that. On the tape she said to the class, "I hear some nice conversation, 'Mary needs three more,' that's what I like to hear." She prefers to have the children close to her, so she can reach out and touch them. That physical closeness, with kids grouped at her feet or sitting snugly together for show-and-tell, seems to provide reassurance as well as to facilitate their learning from each other. In Marcia's view, "Kids are very sensitive to each other. You have to build some of it."

Without even seeming to realize it, children in this classroom take on a lot of responsibility. They make choices about how they spend their time. They help their classmates. They each have several turns at running show-and-tell during the school year. They bring in their own interests, items from the news, books to read to the class. These practices are empowering, and I saw in this class of little kids what Maher and Tetreault found in feminist classrooms at the college level—an emphasis on helping students to become "learners in charge of their own knowledge" (1994, 7).

There is some evidence (Krupnick 1993) that suggests that a tighter structure is necessary in order to achieve equity in a classroom setting. Rosemary was responding to this when she took on the role of the "baddy" in assigning desks and in controlling who speaks. Marcia had started the year with assigned seats at tables (there are no individual desks in her classroom), but by the spring the children had moved about, and no one seemed to be sitting where their fancy name tags, tattered but still sticking from September, had been placed. Most of the time the groups were made up of both boys and girls. Sometimes there was an all-boy or all-girl table for a while, but there was never any labeling of it or rigid separatism. In Marcia's classroom, as in Rosemary's, gender did not seem to be such a big deal. Marcia frequently assigned boy/girl pairs to work on assignments or projects. One time she assigned ad hoc pairs that were all girl/boy combinations. She said she hadn't noticed that. She'd been thinking of two kids who could work together, and one of them had to be a good writer.

The "cubbies" that the kids used to hold their stuff were pink and blue plastic boxes. The colors were used indiscriminately; some boys had pink; some girls had blue. I've known boys who would reject anything pink out of hand. Marcia's cubbies struck me as an illustration of how distinctions with no inherent meaning, like pink and blue, get invested with a partic-ular meaning. But if you don't happen to know these meanings or give them significance, their actual lack of meaning is exposed.

In a math trading game, where kids could bid for objects that Marcia had on display, both girls and boys chose posters of kittens and bunnies and football heroes. And Leroy, in the show-and-tell session described previously, didn't get any teasing when he mentioned learning how to iron his pants, a thing Rosemary's brothers, for instance, never learned how to do.

Although in all three case-study classrooms the teachers were aware and concerned about the problem of airtime and *meant* to alternate be-tween girls and boys, it was only in this classroom, when the children were in charge, that the boy/girl alternation was strictly observed. When Rodrigo was the leader of show-and-tell, one of his pals waved his hand eagerly to be called on, but Rodrigo reminded him, "I can't call on you. I have to call on a girl." Toward the end of the session, when there were several boys with their hands up, he asked, "Any more girls?" before call-ing on two boys in a row.

This arrangement, which had been the kids' idea, was extended from show-and-tell to other areas. One day Matt brought in a guitar and in-sisted on the same alternating scheme, as the kids took turns playing it. The children complained one afternoon when Marcia called mostly on the girls to take turns playing the recorder for the group. On another occasion the kids came back from art with birds they had made. Nicole, the student teacher, let the kids show their birds. She called on two girls in a row and was immediately challenged. She explained she called on a first grade girl and a second grade girl and would then do the same for the boys. These kids, like Rosemary's, have an expectation of fair treatment and felt they had the right to protest when they were not getting it.

Marcia identified Zenia and Harriet as the feminists in her class.

> *Marcia:* Because they're very independent, and they kind of know what they want to do. And I can see them like not going with the status quo. And that's what I look at as being feminist. "I'm doing this because this is what I want to do. Whether it's appropriate for a female or not, this is what I want to do." Harriet has her own little agenda. Zenia's agenda is more around what she wants to do, and she really shows that, and the academic ability is there. Like today with the elephant story, I think Zenia wrote three additional pages.

The qualities Marcia mentions here in these feminist children—inde-pendence, self-directedness, resistance to the status quo—again show an overlap between the way she structures her open classroom and her feminism.

Inner and Outer Worlds

The outside of Marcia's school seemed forbidding, the inside warm and welcoming. The inner geometry was broken up—compared for instance with the long corridors in Rosemary's school. The Ridley School seemed built on a human, even a child's, scale, but its coziness depended on those encircling walls, with few entrances or windows.

The building, like a fortress with limited access, appeared at first to be purposefully cut off from the outside world—not only, it seemed to me, from the possibility of violence in the immediate neighborhood, but also from the underlying violence of a racist society. For security reasons, the teachers themselves did not have keys to the building but had to be let in. If they came in early in the morning, as Marcia liked to do, they rang the bell and, once in, they had to wait near the door to let the next person in, before they could go on to their rooms. Then that second person would wait for the next. This arrangement, based on personal recognizance, seemed very secure, but it was also, in Marcia's opinion, quite tedious.

The classroom windows were small. Of the two windows in Marcia's room, one was frosted. Because of the angles in the room, you had to walk over close to the open window in order to see out. There was a large skylight that let in plenty of light, but of course it was too high to look out of. Moreover, it couldn't be opened, even on hot spring afternoons. After two break-ins in which the thieves apparently came in through a skylight that had been left unlocked, all the skylights had been permanently sealed—an uncomfortable cost of security. Of all the rooms in the school, only the cafeteria had large windows. These faced onto the paved playground, which was half enclosed by the angles of the school. The result was a very inward-looking school structure.

The difficulty in looking out was particularly apparent on May 10, 1994, the day of a solar eclipse. Marcia mentioned to me that some schools in the city were not letting their kids out at recess for fear that they would look at the sun. Marcia's kids were apprehensive. "Don't look at the sun!" they would yell if anyone went close to the one unfrosted window. Marcia had been ambivalent about the eclipse, but eventually she decided to take her kids out in small groups. She showed them how to make a projection through a pinhole. The children hadn't had much of an introduction to the eclipse, but looking at the tiny image they pronounced it "Fresh!"

Although both the fortress-like building and the small-windowed classroom seemed confining on occasion, they could also feel safe and cozy. It would have been easy, I felt, in this classroom of little children in a dangerous city to leave it at that, to close the door, to provide safety and warmth and fun and learning—a sufficient challenge in itself—and to forget about the outside world. Marcia was not satisfied with that, however.

In many ways she made conscious connections between what went on in her classroom and the world outside, the world of danger and experience.

The outside world—the out-of-doors world, the neighborhood and community, the broader and more distant world of news and events—came into the classroom in different ways. One way was by means of show-and-tell, which served like Rosemary's current events as a forum for discussing the news. During the spring of 1994, the end of legal apartheid in South Africa and the election of Nelson Mandela were in the news. Nathan, a first grader who listened to the radio with his parents every morning, would regularly update his classmates. These were historic events for the whole world, and they seemed of immediate interest to the children in Marcia's class. On election day in South Africa, Nathan pointed out that his father had the same T-shirt that Marcia was wearing, which featured a picture of Mandela on the front. Then Rene observed that the quotation on the T-shirt—"Free at last!"—was a quotation from Dr. Martin Luther King Jr. Marcia had posters of Mandela and King and Sojourner Truth in her classroom, reminding the children of the ongoing struggle for freedom of Black people.

Much that the children brought in through show-and-tell had to do with family and neighborhood life, and they also brought up issues of violence and safety. When Raina told about a boy in her church who was in a bike accident, Marcia led a discussion of bike helmets and safety. Rene reported on a parked car that got hit in front of his house the night before. Marcia asked him, "You were up that late?" Rene answered quickly that it was the crash that had awakened him. Matt told about a girl in the news who brought a knife that looked like a lipstick tube to school; the girl got kicked out.

Marcia brought up issues of safety and violence also. Sometimes these were suggested by a memo from the office, but she said this is important and she would deal with it anyway. One day there was a story in the local paper about a grandmother who was shot as she waited for her seven-year-old grandson who was just getting off the school bus. This led to a discussion of drive-by shootings. Marcia asked the children what they should do if they heard the sound of bullets. They knew; they had practiced this earlier in the year. Now again they hunkered down on the floor, making themselves as compact and small a target as possible. They took it very seriously.

This question of being caught in the crossfire was not a remote one but a present danger. It was the reason Marcia had stopped taking her kids to a large park only a few blocks away. She said they used to go all the time, but last year a woman was shot just down the street as she picked up her child from school. After that, more police were posted in the neighborhood, and there was a detective around the school all the time. Recently the police found a man with a gun on the roof of the apartment building across from the school. In these circumstances it does not seem safe to walk along the streets with a line of kids. Marcia does take her kids for walks nearer the school, however. She feels that the immediate neighborhood is safe.

The kids' conversation, as in the show-and-tell session described earlier, indicated that they spent time outdoors after school, riding their bikes in their neighborhood, going shopping with their parents, or going to the park to play. Nathan offered a bit of nature observation in show-and-tell, by describing a squirrel he had seen in the park. He was intensely involved in the details, using his hands to show how the squirrel used its front paws to hold a nut as it ate. He couldn't think of the word *acorn*, but Deshi supplied it.

The class went on a field trip while I was there—to see the workings of a movie theater. This had all been arranged by Nicole, the student teacher. The kids were very excited. In the bus on the way they pointed out their own homes, their friends' homes, the different centers and places where they took tennis lessons or played basketball, the places where their parents worked.

The theater was part of a university program. Nicole introduced us to several fellow students at the theater, all of whom were White. As we were lining up to leave, an African American student came in, and one of the children asked, "Who's this?" All of the children turned around to say hello. They seemed to be particularly drawn to the older student, who was a Black man in this largely White atmosphere.

When we got back to the classroom, we were starving, as we had been ever since we smelled the popcorn in the theater. We learned we had to wait twenty-five minutes for *third* lunch at 12:45. A few kids sprawled on the floor, then Marcia told them all to lie down, and she would read to them. They heaped themselves together on the carpet, listening quietly. She read Dr. Seuss's *Oh, the Places You'll Go!* (1990). In this context it seemed to me to read like a cautionary tale, all about places where it would or would not be safe to go.

There were many visitors to the school, another compensation for its being so enclosed. While I was there the students saw a puppet show and heard a stringed-bass player and a teller of folktales. In Marcia's opinion, these visits all required thank-you notes, which served the purpose of emphasizing manners, reciprocity, and community obligation, and at the same time provided an opportunity for "writing for real purposes," to use a phrase of the Writing Process movement.

There were other visitors. Several groups of teachers came by to observe briefly. That happened so frequently that Marcia told me laughingly, "I just ignore them." Once when a group of observers had some questions, she did make time to talk with them. Nicole and an intern were in the room when I was there in the spring and two more student teachers were expected the next fall. Then there were visits from former students and parents and of course the telephone. Marcia's classroom sometimes lost that enclosed feeling and seemed instead like a busy little center of the world.

Teacher as "Othermother"

In connection with Marcia's story of her life, I used Patricia Hill Collins's term *othermother* to characterize her role in the community and in the school. Collins's discussion of the othermother reveals the multifaceted involvement of such women in the community and the power that gives them.

> Such power is transformative in that Black women's relationships with children and other vulnerable community members is not intended to dominate or control. Rather, its purpose is to bring people along, to—in the word of late–nineteenth-century Black feminists—"uplift the race" so that vulnerable members of the community will be able to attain the self-reliance and independence essential for resistance. (1991, 132)

The othermother "brings along" vulnerable people like children. In this effort she is not only loving and caring, she is also demanding and holds others up to a high standard. The high standard is necessary, because, looking ahead, she sees the need for her students "to attain the self-reliance and independence essential for resistance." In the following passage, both of these aspects of othermothering are apparent. Marcia is talking about her relationships with the African American boys in her class.

> *Marcia:* I think because I'm African American I can talk to them in a way that maybe someone who wasn't African American would be very uncomfortable. I'll say things like, "Can't you be *proud* of what you're doing—what you need to do—because you're Black?" And, "I want you to do well because I like to see Black males do well." Now that could also be said by someone who wasn't Afro-American, but sometimes I wonder if my saying that makes them feel a lot more like, "I gotta do this or I want to do this or I should do this because of my teacher, who has said to me that I need to do this because she cares."

Marcia goes on to contrast this approach to what she has sometimes seen in colleagues who are not African American.

> *Marcia:* Now that again might be my interpretation of looking at children sometimes as taking advantage of someone who is of another ethnic background, because the person tends to feel that, "I need to be good to these little

kids because everything in their life is so miserable." And I do find that a lot with my colleagues who are not of African American background. I feel this way, but then on the other hand I try not to show it in my dealing with them or their parents.

Carla: You try not to show that you're feeling—

Marcia: I feel so sorry for them. Because that way it's like a sympathetic feeling, and they take advantage of it.

Carla: The kids do?

Marcia: The kids *and parents* do.

Here Marcia makes a distinction between a "sympathetic feeling," which seems to get in the way and tempt the teacher to relax her standards for the child she pities. Marcia feels sorry for some of her kids, too, but she "tries not to show it," because she is still going to hold high standards of behavior and achievement for that child.

Marcia's stance toward the parents of her students is similar. She knows these parents, she had them as kids; she teaches them now in adult education courses; she knows them in the community. Some of them, she says, are very young, inexperienced, exhausted, and overwhelmed.

Marcia: If you decide, "OK, I'm not going to demand that the parent comes up to school because she has all these little babies at home, and she's on welfare, and she's struggling, or she's having problems with her husband and she just can't get up here." Where I say, "Look, bring the babies and come up here." They [White teachers] might do that but then I find some people don't because they feel, "Oh my gosh, you can't do this." My whole thing is, "Fine, you have these babies, you have problems with your husband, but I'm having problems with your son, and I need to talk with you and your son and see if we can work something out."

Carla: Yeah, so you think of that more in relation with the boys that you have?

Marcia: Yeah, but I do the same thing with the girls too. I have a little girl who I feel is not doing well, and her mom has five children, but I demand she comes up and we sit and we talk. I listen to her concerns about how she's overwhelmed with the children and her house, and I do feel for her, but I don't let her know, and I still demand from her, you know, "You need to sit with this child." And I even tried to talk with her about, "You need to put some of the children in an after school program, so you can have more time with the younger ones." You know, just trying to say, "No matter what, you've got to work with these children. No matter what, no matter if you're overwhelmed, you've got to help each child some."

Here Marcia is clearly "bringing along" the parents of her children as well. With them too she feels a sympathy that she does not let interfere with her ideas of what the parents need to do. As she does with her students, she makes her expectations clear to the parents and is emphatic about how they must help their children "no matter what."

Marcia thinks of these issues in long-range terms. There is a cycle that needs to be broken.

> *Marcia:* Yeah, but somehow you have to start doing that, because I look at some children who might say, "My grandmother grew up in the projects, my mom had me, I'm having a baby. We've got four generations, and nobody's finished high school." How is that, say, fourth generation child going to survive? And, you know, you see that, I see that in my room. I see it.
>
> *Carla:* Do you feel that, when you see that coming, that gives you an extra impetus to stand behind that child and push that child?
>
> *Marcia:* And sometime push Mom.
>
> *Carla:* And push Mom?
>
> *Marcia:* Yeah, I feel like now I have to push Mom because with the age child I got, Mom has a lot to do with how this child is going to do.

The logic of the othermother is apparent in this passage. She must look beyond the child in her room and work with the parents and the wider community in order to help that child. At the same time she is trying to ensure the child's survival, his or her "self-reliance and independence essential for resistance," as Collins put it. Marcia, like Collins, is concerned about the child not only as an individual but as a person needed by the community for its own continuity and transformation.

Like all teachers, Marcia had to superintend the whole class and pay attention to the individual child simultaneously. The following videotaped vignette shows her doing that:

> The children gather back together in the large group, and Marcia gives them some word problems. She first connects this with a story Matt had told in show-and-tell—a trick story but like a word problem—it gives it a fun connection, and the group seems to enjoy working out the problems and responding.
>
> Derrick, who sports a single earring, is sitting right by her knee. She placed him there because of some mischief that I didn't see. After Marcia reads one of the math problems, Derrick starts counting on his fingers—held up in front of his face—completely absorbed, counting very slowly, losing track, and starting all over again. His intense face is caught in the frame of the videotape. The class rolls on, a child gives the answer, Marcia poses another problem. Finally, Derrick reaches the end of his calculations. Exultantly he calls out his answer, "SEVEN!" By then, Marcia is talking about something else entirely, but you know that she still managed to hear Derrick, because on the tape you can see a disembodied hand appear and pat him on the head.

Marcia had said she liked the children close to her so she could reach out and touch them. Here her gesture, like a blessing, served as a reminder to Derrick that he mattered, his diligence was appreciated, and that what he said was heard, even if the class had moved ahead three problems.

The idea of the othermother assumes a community that she taps in to for the benefit of her children. In Marcia's case, she lived in the immediate geographic community and knew her kids' parents in many contexts. She saw them regularly at church and in the various adult education programs she was involved in. She knew where they lived, and she understood the challenges and joys of their lives.

An additional benefit of this community orientation for the children is that they have a sense of their own place within the community. When Marcia told Lawrence about seeing his aunt at church, she did not need to say, "You'd better watch out. I'll tell your aunt if you misbehave or don't do your work well." The implications are stronger and subtler than that. It's a reminder to the child—all of the children because they could all hear this exchange—that they are part of a community. What they are doing in school is important, so important that the adult world is interested. At the same time they are being "brought along" so that they can take part in the community as self-reliant and resistant persons, who, like those of Marcia's students who themselves became teachers, can in turn help in the preservation and transformation of the community.

NOTES

1. The first Black player in the American League. I missed this name and the significance of the reference; I asked her later.

2. This phone, necessary for E-mail, caused the occasional interruption, but it was important to Marcia's life in that classroom. It was liberating, too. She never had to struggle to get to an office phone when it was free, as most teachers do. In fact, my experiences in this classroom made me think how infantilizing it is that most teacher do *not* have phones in their rooms.

3. Benjamin Spock, *Baby and Child Care*.

5

Three Teachers

Now we must recognize differences among women who are our equals, neither inferior nor superior, and devise ways to use each others' difference to enrich our vision and our joint struggles.

—Audre Lorde

In the first chapter of this book I set out some of the questions that the teachers in this study would be dealing with. I presented these as questions feminism raises about education. I saw these questions as changing over time—changing because different people in different circumstances were doing the asking—but also as ongoing and overlapping. I claimed that feminist theory would be helpful in interpreting practice. It would disclose underlying ideas, pose questions that teachers need to ask about our practice and our selves, and open up our thoughts to new possibilities. Throughout the case studies I have tried to show the ways a feminist analysis can be applied to the lives and work of elementary school teachers. As I warned, this study would not come up with clear, single answers to any of these complex questions, but rather would show a variety of responses to common issues. The thinking and practice of these teachers offer some powerful and generative models.

In this last chapter I want to place the three case-study teachers next to each other and look at what they have in common, where they differ, how they deal with the questions feminism raises about teaching, and what we can learn from them.

I found many similarities among the three case-study teachers. Some of these were merely incidental but seemed nevertheless to draw connections among the teachers across the three studies. For instance, Marcia told me that in her family "you *did* things," which echoed Lucy's words with the same emphasis describing the women in her family as "women who *did* things." Rosemary and Marcia both mentioned power tools as a significant symbol for access to power in their childhood years. Rosemary's "school of aunts" reminded me of Lucy's teacher-aunts.

In their life histories the three teachers looked back on themselves as young girls, thinking about their own lives and observing the adults around them. Rosemary saw how limited her mother's life had been made by "sexism and classism . . . and the power dynamics of marriage." Lucy was impressed by the work of her teacher-aunts. Marcia's mother wanted for her daughter the education and opportunities that she had never had. The three teachers could see the limitations placed on the lives of this older generation of women. As the daughters grew up they sometimes pushed against the boundaries of acceptable female behavior. They dabbled in mischief, climbed trees in Sunday clothes, delivered papers as a "newsgirl," excelled in math, fixed things, and became knowledgeable about sports as they worked out who they were within and outside of these boundaries.

I was surprised to find that each of these three women initially resisted the idea of herself as a teacher. Lucy said, "I never dreamed I'd be a teacher. Heaven forbid! at the time is what I felt, but *they get you in the end!*" Rosemary remembered wondering, "Why would anyone want to teach?" And Marcia, after her student teaching experience, thought, "Never would I teach! No way am I going to look at another classroom!" As they remember it, these women all had serious questions about their move into teaching. Their reluctance seems to reflect a certain amount of resistance to this form of "women's work" and a recognition of the great challenge and historically low status of elementary school teaching in this society.

For each of them—because of the times in which they grew up, because they were women, because of their class and race status, because of financial need—their career options were severely limited. Teaching was one of the few possibilities open to them. None of them talked of other strong ambitions. They might, then, have accepted teaching as a low-status, low-wage, rather grueling job and slogged along through the years or gone on to something else. But they didn't do any of these things. Instead, they found broader meanings in teaching than they had even been able to imagine when they began. In different ways they all came up against and dealt with this compelling question: How could they transform the traditional women's role of teacher so that it could be intellectually and morally satisfying, consistent with their feminist ideas, worthy of their years of devoted service—and so that it could encompass within it the possibilities for continued growth and change?

Underlying these teachers' transformative ability, I believe, is their on-going development of a more conscious practice. From the wisdom of their own practice, they have established the grounds from which they can look critically at the structure of power, interests, and ideology that re-strict their teaching lives and shape the educational system in this coun-try. By these same grounds they have felt empowered to work for change.

They mentioned experiences that contributed to this consciousness: Rosemary read Simone de Beauvoir and realized that she could "question the culture." Lucy discovered the profound sexism in her daughter's reading book. Marcia worked with other teachers in establishing an alter-native, open school. Their stories also revealed more current experiences from which they are still learning and changing, such as Lucy's struggles with Reggie, Rosemary's dealings with her faculty, and Marcia's conflict with the White student teacher in her workshop.

As they told their life stories, the teachers' memories of their girlhood and their growing consciousness connected their own life experiences with the development of their teaching practice. Encounters with sexism, racism, classism, and homophobia influenced their classroom practice and the somewhat different emphases they place on their goals for their students.

Marcia's feminist practice revolved around questions of strength and safety. She wanted her girls to know that they could do anything. The way she let her students run show-and-tell and other classroom activities showed her confidence in their intelligence and their care for each other. Through her reading materials, the images on the walls, and the class-room discussions, she showed her first and second graders "an opposi-tional worldview" in bell hooks's phrase. Marcia wanted all her children to do well, to be proud, to feel the support of their community, and to be future sources of strength for that community.

Rosemary structured her class as a safe place where it is "OK to be who you are." She encouraged her boys to help out in the kindergarten. She helped her class to learn about, accept, and dance with Leonard, the boy with cerebral palsy. She did not tolerate insults or teasing that was based on stereotypes, like "You fag." She outlawed sexist behavior, nipped it in the bud. She was willing to be the "baddy" in requiring boys and girls to sit together. Any sexist, racist, or homophobic remarks or items in the news were important subjects of discussion. She wanted all her children to face and accept their own differences, to withstand those "million little suicides," to find ways to deal with the difficulties of the world, to ques-tion the culture and the curriculum, and in that way to develop an un-derstanding that would help them deal with differences, speak up for themselves and others, and take action.

Lucy established a rich, creative environment for learning in her class-room, where her students could discover and share many things. They had opportunities to be authors, artists, builders, readers, and thinkers. Lucy wanted her girls to have an equal place in this active classroom, and she encouraged them to create their own adventures, to be heroines and "speak-your-own-mind girls." Her class the year I observed showed a greater than usual degree of tension, often around issues of gender and race. Lucy's policy was to let the kids' reactions surface, so that they could be identified and discussed and, if possible, changed. In her open discussions with the kids, she wanted to hear their ideas. She wanted all her children to be involved and productive and to feel "taken care of."

I found that in all three classrooms, seating arrangements seemed to illustrate the teachers' expectations of the way their students ought to relate to each other. All three teachers had their students sitting in groups of three to five children, but they assigned the seats differently. Rosemary always required boys and girls to sit together with the hope, which seemed to be fulfilled, that this would help them get to know and accept each other better. At the beginning of the year, Marcia assigned her students to seats with fancy nametags, but by the time I was there, the name tags were being ignored. Her children moved frequently, the groups forming and reforming around various projects, but the groups were almost always gender-mixed. Lucy placed boys and girls in mixed groups half the time; the other half of the time the kids themselves could choose, and the result was gender segregation.

It was surprising to me that even these consciously feminist teachers did not always give equal time to girls, and in the end the kid-run show-and-tell seemed to be the most egalitarian. I've discussed some of the obstacles in the way of consistently equalizing airtime—the difficulty of keeping track, the pressure of other needs, the internalized expectations that make the discussion appear to the teacher to be more equal than it is. On the other hand, I found it frustrating to observe this imbalance. Equal time seems such a simple, basic thing, but it turns out to be quite revolutionary, so against the grain, so counter to our everyday assumptions about the world that it would seem to stand our culture on its head to insist on equality for females, even in these microcosmic worlds.

In addition to these questions of stereotyping and equality, many aspects of teaching practice that I observed seemed to be in response to questions of how to make school a better fit for girls, for children of color, and for children who are poor. The practice of the three teachers was not based on indoctrination, competitiveness, the mere transmission of information, or an overemphasis on test results. As feminist teachers—with different emphases—they saw their role in terms of helping their students to learn and grow, to think for themselves, to understand and accept each other, and to work together.

All three teachers had been involved in curricular change and innovation in many subjects. In particular, they all worked to revise and expand their math programs. This interest in math was both explicitly and implicitly connected with the current discussion of girls and math and with an awareness that girls do less well in this area and feel less confident. These teachers have written grants, attended and taught workshops and courses, tried out and demonstrated new materials. Their math curricula use intriguing, hands-on materials and emphasize thinking, reasoning, explaining, cooperating, and applying math concepts. Some aspects of the math I observed could be seen as projects that relate math more directly to girls' experience, such as Lucy's discussion of fractions, Marcia's "family" metaphor, or Rosemary's Quilt Squares. The hands-on, cooperative, discussion-based approach to math in all three rooms is consistent with the recommendations in the American Association of University Women's report for strategies to improve girls' achievement and interest in math (1992, 52) and the findings of Myra Sadker and David Sadker (1994).

The three teachers transformed the traditional curriculum in an effort to incorporate different voices and a broader worldview. Marcia's classroom was full of images from a diverse world of color. The value she placed on Black culture, history, family, and community not only disrupted traditional White education but created a new curriculum. Lucy gave play to the voices in her diverse group by the emphasis she placed on the children's writing, drawing, publishing of books, and working in clay and with blocks. The children chose their own reading from a purposefully diverse selection of books. They did not use textbooks. Rosemary used textbooks in some subjects—sometimes rather outdated ones. In one instance that I observed she helped her students raise questions about the unidimensional worldview presented in their schoolbooks.

All three teachers handled discipline in a way that showed their fundamental respect and care for their students. The classroom rules and expectations were subjects for discussion in meetings of the whole class, and students' ideas were honored. Within these parameters there were vivid contrasts in handling discipline issues. Marcia would take a student aside for a "talking to," or alternatively she would stand straight and tall, looking down at the child and making sure the child knew what she required or how he or she had not lived up to expectations, "Now what did Miss Roberts *say* about cutting in line?" Rosemary, being short, could meet her fifth graders eye to eye. She tended to treat them nearly as equals, using jokes and relying on her strong rapport with them in getting them to behave. "It's never me against them," she said, banging her fists together to illustrate what she meant. Lucy would typically bend or sit down to get on the same level with the child or group of children. She would talk and listen carefully, trying to get them to express their ideas and understand what had happened. She wanted to bring their ideas to the surface so they could be understood and dealt with.

The question of discipline and authority had a special place in this study, because this is and has been a problematic area for many women teachers. It is also the crux of the issue for teachers who must exert their power in order to change the sexist, racist, and classist ideas and behavior that their children inevitably bring with them into the classroom.

In all of these classrooms the issue of safety was an important one. Sometimes classrooms are the safest places in children's lives—the most secure and the most predictable. There is threat in the streets, and violence comes into the home via the television. Sometimes the homes themselves are not safe but are places of abuse, neglect, confusion, and desperation. I heard terrible stories from all three teachers about the lives of some of their students. Every teacher knows such stories and needs to know as well the importance of her room as a safe haven and herself as a source of strength for her students.

Rosemary stressed the idea of safety in connection with the sexism, racism, and homophobia of this society. She saw the connection between sexism and the homophobia that keeps gender stereotypes in place. She wanted her kids to feel safe in being themselves. Marcia had to take another degree of safety into account because of the area in which her school is located and the need for children to know how to protect themselves—to know where it is safe to go and how to hit the ground when they hear gunfire. In her emphasis on safety, Marcia worked to develop the children's own strength and knowledge, in addition to protecting them. In Lucy's class safety was a burning issue that year, because she was dealing with the "class from hell." In fact some of her children did not feel physically safe with their classmates, and some did get hurt while I was there. Lucy struggled with the question of how to make all of her children feel taken care of.

Through their different approaches to discipline, all three case-study teachers needed to keep order in their classrooms, but they also sought to empower their students. They gave them responsibility by letting them lead the class, direct show-and-tell, talk from the lectern, help other kids, voice their own opinions, and work together. They honored their students' ideas by listening carefully and letting them share their ideas with the whole class. In each setting, the structured times when the class talked together with the teacher seemed to be important moments for seeing the teachers' efforts to carry out their feminist understandings and goals.

In Lucy's story meetings she would read to the children, and then they would all talk about the story and discuss related issues. At other times the children would talk about what they did during vacation or the fact that they got something new. Lucy led them in candid discussions about their feelings and reactions—why Tom acts as he does, whether Neil is funny or not, how Brianna could try to make friends. This way of making it possible for the children to connect their outside experiences and their personal feelings to what is going on in school, which all three teachers made part of the curriculum, reflects feminist ideas of the relevance of the personal and affective to knowledge and learning.

Show-and-tell in Marcia's room included a broad range of interests. It was also a vehicle for the empowerment of students in that they not only participated in, but took charge of, this daily event. Marcia held frequent discussions of behavior with an emphasis on how to behave in school. Additionally, the life in this classroom was explicitly related to the outside world of the community; issues of self-defense and survival were central, as were possibilities for contributing to the community.

Some of the discussions in Rosemary's class dealt with personal topics, like dreams. Others focused on a critical examination of curricular materials or items in the news. Rosemary helped her students look for points of connection between the curriculum or the news and their own lives— and to question the culture.

In these ways a teacher, even a teacher of young children, can empower her students by helping them deal with and resist racism, sexism, homophobia, and classism. Our society finds many ways of keeping us "all in our places," of telling a girl or a child of color that she or he can't do that. The teacher needs to find ways of saying, "You can."

These issues seem to have brought us a long way from "gender issues in the classroom," although they arise from the initial question of what we believe are the differences between women and men, boys and girls. The concerns of these feminist teachers encompass the whole child. Differences of gender, race, class, ability, and other subject positions are all interconnected. The teachers focus on the reality of these children in their classrooms today but also keep in mind the growing child, the future for that child, and the future of our society.

In these case studies I have chosen to show what these feminist teachers *do* in their diverse contexts and have resisted generalizing or extracting rules of behavior from their practice or labeling their feminism. Like Maher and Tetreault, I found that the diversity of these three classrooms and the complexity of the issues I found there moved me "away from pedagogical generalizations towards the telling of particular stories" (1994, 15). In many cases the teacher's reactions are context-specific or the inspiration of the moment and not generalizable.

But I also feel a certain obligation, since I have been in the position of a clock stopper. If what can be learned from a careful analysis of practice is to have any usefulness, there must be some way for teachers to think about these things *before* they occur in the classroom. We won't always have the opportunity for reflection in the real time of classroom life.

This is a matter of some urgency, which my experience as an observer of these classrooms—and more specifically as a researcher forced to confront some of my own assumptions and blind spots—has made clear. We must work to discover who we are and where these assumptions, blind spots, stereotypes, and prejudices come from. It can be a shock to discover the extent of what we have not seen. Peggy McIntosh reports from her experience of working with teachers, "It is traumatically shocking to white women teachers in particular to realize that we were not only trained but were as teachers unwittingly training others to overlook, reject, exploit, disregard, or be at war with most people in the world. One feels hood winked and also sick at heart at having been such a vehicle for racism, misogyny, upper class power and militarism" (1989).

How have we become "such a vehicle" and how can we transform ourselves? One of the projects of feminism, as well as of other liberatory movements, has been to question knowledge that has claimed to be neutral, objective, and universal and to show that such knowledge often comes from and shows distinctive marks of being White, male, and otherwise privileged. As Sandra Harding points out in *Whose Science? Whose Knowledge?* (1991), it is people—flesh and blood human beings—who do science and create knowledge. It "starts from" somewhere, and it makes a difference where.

School knowledge is most often based on the same androcentric, or male-centered, epistemologies with the same assumptions about the world. Given new challenges from women, people of color, Third World peoples, gay and lesbian people, the poor, persons with disabilities, and other oppressed groups, this androcentric worldview is justifiably under attack. Knowledge comes from many sources. In this study I have tried to "start from" teachers' lives, as a group whose voices are not often heard, but whose thinking and insight are important in making needed changes.

Another project of feminism is to urge us to work toward a more *conscious* practice, in which we are increasingly aware of the unquestioned assumptions we carry with us, the "hidden curriculum," the implications of what we say and do, the dangers of misunderstanding, and the importance of different voices. As Lisa Delpit warned, "We do not really see through our eyes or hear through our ears but through our beliefs" (1995, 46). She was speaking of the stark need for a teacher to recognize her own assumptions, to see through her own beliefs, in order to hear what someone else is saying. In other words, it is not a clear pane of glass through which we are looking at the world, and we need to identify the scratches, the whorls, and the imperfections.

I hope the following suggestions will help our efforts toward a more conscious practice. I have put the suggestions in the form of "things to think about," or questions that feminism—broadly understood, as in this study—has to ask about our world of teaching and the wider world as well. My study has not come up with a best way of handling these complicated issues, though the three case-study teachers in many instances have provided helpful, challenging, and often inspiring ideas and practices. What follows are some questions I think we, as teachers, should keep asking ourselves:

1. What are my own ideas about gender, race, class, and sexual orientation? How can I examine these ideas and assumptions, knowing how powerfully they affect my teaching and my relationships with my students?
2. Do I let my students *know* that issues of equity and justice—gender, race, sexuality, class—are important to me? Or does my practice sometimes unintentionally suggest that I collude with prevailing stereotypes?
3. Do I consistently challenge students' (not just my own students') use of stereotypes and their name-calling, like *fag, sissy, lezzy*? Do I model intolerance for prejudice, so students can follow, like Rosemary's student Lydia, who criticized the sub for making a racist remark?
4. How equal is my treatment of my students? Do I really give them equal airtime, equal teacher attention, and equal access to the resources of the classroom?
5. What do the seating arrangements and other group formations in my classroom suggest about the way I want different kids, like boys and girls, to relate? Should I offer a choice or be "the baddy" and make such decisions for them?
6. Do the choices I make about books, units, themes, classroom decorations, and discussion topics reflect a unitary, White, androcentric vision of the world? How can my curriculum make way for new voices and new possibilities?
7. Do all my students both talk *and* listen? Both of these activities are too central to education for us to leave them to chance. How can I get the quieter ones to speak up, the more talkative to listen?
8. What kind of forum does my classroom offer for the exchange of ideas, what opportunities are there for students to bring in their own pressing interests, their fears and joys? How do I value what they bring? In what ways do they learn from each other, as well as from me? How do I learn from them?

9. How safe do the children—*all* the children—feel in my classroom—
   physically safe, safe from the pain of discrimination, and safe in
   their own growing strength and understanding? How can I make
   room for diversity and growth and struggle, while still making my
   students feel safe and cared for?

10. How well do I listen—*really* listen, with Delpit's emphasis—to the
    understanding and input of parents and other community mem-
    bers?

11. How can I help students deal with life outside of and after school,
    their future, and their lives in the community? What kind of under-
    standing *now* can help them survive, speak up for themselves, sup-
    port each other, and work together for a better world?

By posing these as questions that teachers need to ask ourselves, I certainly do not mean to imply that the burden of change lies only with teachers or that teachers themselves can transform our current educational system, which is in such need of fundamental change. Our country needs to
question our goals, structures, curricula, and testing systems at the most
profound level, and to imagine what schools might be like with very different values at their core, as Nel Noddings has done in *The Challenge to
Care in Schools* (1992) and Jane Roland Martin in *Schoolhome* (1992).
Changes of this magnitude cannot rest only with teachers, but I have come
to realize, from my own experience in the course of this project, the urgent
need to change ourselves. We can start this effort by finding the knowledge
our society has led us to ignore—Toni Morrison's "well bred instinct
against noticing"—and seeing how it reflects back on ourselves. Such an
effort is crucial so that we are not, to repeat Peggy McIntosh's warning,
"unwittingly training others to overlook, reject, exploit, disregard, or be at
war with most people in the world." The questions we need to ask ourselves are painful, and it is extremely difficult to make the changes we
need in our ideas and in our practice. In a sense these are the very questions we are not supposed to ask—if we are to remain "all in our places."

I mentioned at the beginning of this book that some of the people I approached early in this project thought that "feminist elementary school
teacher" was a contradiction in terms. Sandra Harding (1991) and other
feminist writers have pointed out that during much of our history and
still today the phrases *woman scientist* and *woman knower* have similarly
been seen as contradictions in terms. The contradictions reveal the place
we were "meant" to occupy—loving but uncritical teacher, docile
woman—and hint at what might happen if we break out of the box, refuse
that identity, see through the ideology and structures of our society that
have shaped us and have put us in our "places."

Harding calls for developing a "traitorous identity," whereby we *choose* an identity that contradicts the one we were born into or find ourselves in: Those of us who are men can nevertheless be feminists, those who are White can be antiracist, those who are straight can be against homophobia, and those who are elementary school teachers can be thinkers and knowers.

Elementary school teachers have knowledge that we need for the transformation of education. Their world, as I illustrated in the preface to this book, is not well understood by those who stand outside it. Too often what teachers know, the knowledge they have gained from their practice, from their experience, and from their reflection, is not valued where decisions are made. For the most part, school administrators, state departments of education, textbook writers, standardized test makers, and those who market these products are far away from the experience inside a classroom. Yet test makers in some far-off city can drive the curriculum in our local schools, while the knowledge of teachers is passed over.

Teachers, as we saw in the work of Marcia, Lucy, and Rosemary, have influence that extends throughout their schools and into the wider community. And in their own classrooms, although they are hemmed about with demands and restrictions, teachers essentially create the environment in which their students spend the day—the attitude toward learning, the angle on the curriculum, the development of rules, the growth of relationships, and the assumptions about other people. In other words, as teachers, we powerfully affect the way the world looks to our students.

Our students do not fit "all in their places," and neither do we. In redefining the work of teachers, we need to find room for our own experience, practice, and reflection. Educators outside the classroom must also listen to and act upon the knowledge of teachers, as we all work together toward the transformation of education.

Appendix A

Preliminary Interview

Questions in the preliminary interview were aimed at exploring the teachers' feminist ideas and getting a sense of how they believed their feminism affected their work. I arranged to arrive an hour before the end of school so that I could observe the class briefly, which would give me some context for discussing with each teacher her feminism and practice.

After thanking the teacher for letting me come and talking a bit about the class I had just observed, I described my project and told more about myself, my teaching, and my goals for this study.

Then I asked the following questions, with some variation:

1. How long have you been teaching? How long have you been at this school? What grades? What is it like teaching here? [Compare with other schools if appropriate.] How would you characterize your relations with the principal? How about relations with other teachers?
2. Do you think other teachers see you as a feminist? How so? How do they react? Are there other feminist teachers here in your school? How do you describe yourself as a feminist? What does being a feminist mean to you? When and how did you become a feminist?
3. How do you think being a feminist affects your teaching? Can you give me some examples? What do you think would be a good example of a time your plans or reactions were affected by your feminist beliefs? What about the opposite—a time when, as a teacher, you had to act in a way that went against your feminist beliefs?

4. Are there any other questions that came up for you in this conversation? Do you think you would be willing to have me do a case study in your classroom? This is what I have in mind. [Talk about the schedule.]

Originally I expected to conduct ten preliminary interviews, and then, after these were completed and analyzed, choose three teachers who would show some variation in terms of six specific dimensions I had identified: the teacher's feminist ideas; her teaching style; the grade she taught; her age and length of teaching experience; the social class and race variation within the class; and the leadership style in the school as a whole. The plan of starting with ten preliminary interviews was abandoned, however, when I met Lucy, who was my fourth interview. I decided (for reasons that I discuss in the chapter about Lucy) to start with her as my first case study. From then on I switched back and forth between "preliminary" interviews and ongoing work with the case-study teachers.

Appendix B

Interview Guides

The questions in these guides are open-ended. There were some questions I wanted to be sure to ask every teacher, but I also felt free to follow tangents in the conversation. I would already have answers to some of these questions from previous conversations.

1. *Life History Interview:*
    Today I'd like to ask you some questions that have to do with your history as a teacher and a feminist.
    1. Looking back, how would you describe yourself as a student?
    2. Will you tell me a bit about yourself growing up and your family? Where did you grow up? What did your parents do for work? How many brothers and sisters do you have?
    3. Do you remember incidents or things that were said while you were growing up that made you think there were things you couldn't do because you were a girl? Do you remember how you reacted? What significance does that memory have for you now?
    4. How did you decide to become a teacher? Were there any other careers you considered? [Follow up on any connections between this decision and gender.]
    5. When would you say you became a feminist? What happened? [depending on timing] Did this affect your decision to become a teacher/your teaching? In your teacher training did you have any courses or parts of courses about gender and teaching?
    6. Do you think your feminist ideas, the way you think of yourself as a feminist, have changed since that time? How so? How have these changes affected your teaching?

7. I realized preparing these questions that these were all *my* questions—they related to my experience of teaching and feminism. When you think of your teaching and your feminism, what do you think I've left out? What other questions would you ask? How would you answer them? [How would I?]

    Sometimes after a conversation like this, you think of something else that would have been relevant—or it might make you think of other questions. I hope if you think of something else about these issues, you'll tell me about it.

2. *The Teacher's Role Interview:*
    Today I'd like to ask you some more questions about your job here at ____ School.
    1. Outside of the classroom, how do you think being a feminist affects your job? Can you give me some examples?
    2. Do you think being a feminist makes you see issues differently, react differently to things going on in the school (outside of the classroom)? Can you give me an example?
    3. Do you think being a feminist affects your relationships with other adults in the school? How so?
    [The following questions have to do with the teacher's autonomy in the classroom and her ability to influence decisions beyond her classroom. If the teacher does not mention these issues as connected with her feminism, I will ask her the following questions about her job—whether or not she sees them as connected to feminism. Again, we will already have discussed some of these issues.]
    1. To what extent can you decide on the units you teach? What texts, units, subjects are you required to teach? Who makes those decisions? How? Any other things you feel obliged to teach? What other factors influence your choices—parents? standardized tests?
    2. What about the schedule—how much control do you have over that? Do you have any input into the specialists' schedules? Could you arrange to team up with another teacher? Have you ever?
    3. How are rules made for this classroom? Do children have input? How are the rules presented to the children? How are they enforced? What sorts of school-wide rules are there? Any you disagree with?
    4. In what ways can you influence decisions made at this school—committees, faculty meetings, access to the principal? What would you do if you had an idea or a criticism you wanted to do something about? Can you give me an example of a time when you did affect a school decision outside of your classroom?

5. How would you characterize the principal's leadership style? How supportive? How does s/he make suggestions for change?
6. Have you ever worked collaboratively with another teacher? What did you do together? How did you arrange time to plan together? What sorts of time do teachers have at this school for meeting together when they can set the agenda?

3. *Sample Questions: Questions for Marcia, 5/23*
[This is an example of a collection of follow-up questions—questions that came up while I typed the transcript or reread my notes.]
What are the little notebooks for? She mentioned them Thursday—notes that the kids had not responded to.
The bass-player with the other classes—19 boys and 3 girls asked questions—what does she think?
Is there a teachers' lunchroom?
Do all the kids participate in show-and-tell? Does she sometimes encourage/restrain, or is it entirely kid-run? How about other years?
She mentioned doing workshops for teachers on "inner city kids." What does she think teachers need to hear?
What child is the most trouble? Is this a particularly "good" class?
Her views of the busing program.
Population of school, parents' occupations.

Appendix C

Data Collection

I spent a month to six weeks collecting the bulk of the data for each case study. During that time I visited the teacher's classroom two or three times a week, usually for the entire school day. After school I interviewed the teacher, if we had so planned, using a tape recorder, or sometimes we just talked. Beyond the original block of time, there were phone conversations, lunches, workshops, and visits to all the teachers' classes the following year.

I took field notes on class activities, focusing on aspects of the teacher's practice that she had identified as influenced by her feminism, and collecting other information that I thought was relevant or that I had questions about. Because I was moving around the classroom, or following the students to lunch or art class, I quite frequently had to remember things until I got a chance to write them down. As soon as possible after a classroom visit, I typed up my expanded field notes—adding as much information as I could remember to what I had written in my notebook. On some occasions significant moments or bits of conversation would occur to me later on, and I would add those too.

I videotaped each class at least once. Videotaping seemed to remove me from the immediacy of the classroom. I would survey the room and select what I wanted to record, but I couldn't hear enough or attend enough to follow all that was going on, and I couldn't take notes at the same time. Being busy with the technology, I was less aware of my own reactions and less apt to have questions for the teacher immediately afterward. Since I was less conscious of what was going on, when I looked at the tape later on, there were always some surprises. Thus the videotaping did provide some useful information.

Bibliography

Alton-Lee, Adrienne, and Graham Nuthall. 1993. Reframing Classroom Research: A Lesson from the Private World. *Harvard Educational Review* 63, 1: 50–84.

American Association of University Women. 1992. *The AAUW Report: How Schools Shortchange Girls.* Washington, D.C.: American Association of University Women Educational Foundation.

Ballenger, Cynthia. 1992. Because You Like Us: The Language of Social Control. *Harvard Educational Review* 62, 2: 199–208.

Belenky, Mary F., Blythe M. Clinchy, Nancy R. Goldberger, and Jill M. Tarule. 1986. *Women's Ways of Knowing: The Development of Self, Voice, and Mind.* New York: Basic Books.

Biklen, Sari Knopp. 1995. *School Work: Gender and the Cultural Construction of Teaching.* New York: Teachers College Press.

Bogdan, Robert, and Sari Knopp Biklen. 1982. *Qualitative Research for Education.* Boston: Allyn and Bacon.

Bronte, Charlotte. 1971. *Villette.* Boston: Houghton Mifflin.

Casey, Kathleen. 1993. *I Answer with My Life: Life Histories of Women Working for Social Change.* New York: Routledge.

Collins, Patricia Hill. 1991. *Black Feminist Thought: Knowledge, Consciousness, and the Politics of Empowerment.* New York: Routledge.

Cullum, Albert. 1967. *Push Back the Desks.* New York: Citation Press.

Dahl, Raold. 1988. *Matilda.* New York: Puffin.

———. 1982. *BFG.* New York: Puffin.

Davies, Bronwyn. 1993. *Shards of Glass: Children Reading and Writing beyond Gendered Identities.* Cresskill, N.J.: Hampton Press.

de Beauvoir, Simone. 1957. *The Second Sex.* New York: Knopf.

Delpit, Lisa D. 1988. The Silenced Dialogue: Power and Pedagogy in Educating Other People's Children. *Harvard Educational Review* 58, 3: 280–98.

———. 1995. *Other People's Children: Cultural Conflict in the Classroom.* New York: The New Press.

DeVault, Marjorie L. 1990. Talking and Listening from Women's Standpoint: Feminist Strategies for Interviewing and Analysis. *Social Problems* 37, 1: 96–116.

Giddings, Paula. 1984. *When and Where I Enter: The Impact of Black Women on Race and Sex in America.* New York: Bantam.

Gilligan, Carol. 1982. *In a Different Voice: Psychological Theory and Women's Development.* Cambridge, Mass.: Harvard University Press.

Grumet, Madeleine R. 1988. *Bitter Milk: Women and Teaching.* Amherst: University of Massachusetts Press.

Harding, Sandra. 1991. *Whose Science? Whose Knowledge? Thinking from Women's Lives.* Ithaca, N.Y.: Cornell University Press.

Heath, Shirley Brice. 1983. *Ways with Words: Language, Life and Work in Communities and Classrooms.* New York: Cambridge University Press.

Holland, Dorothy C., and Margaret A. Eisenhart. 1990. *Educated in Romance: Women, Achievement, and College Culture.* Chicago: University of Chicago Press.

hooks, bell. 1989. *Talking Back: Thinking Feminist, Thinking Black.* Boston: South End Press.

———. 1994. *Teaching to Transgress: Education as the Practice of Freedom.* New York: Routledge.

Khayatt, Madika Didi. 1992. *Lesbian Teachers: An Invisible Presence.* Albany: SUNY Press.

Kissen, Rita M. 1996. *The Last Closet: The Real Lives of Lesbian and Gay Teachers.* Portsmouth, N.H.: Heinemann.

Kohl, Herbert. 1969. *The Open Classroom: A Practical Guide to a New Way of Teaching.* New York: Vintage.

Krupnick, Catherine. 1993. Meadows College Prepares for Men. In Kenneth Winston and Mary Jo Bane (eds.), *Gender and Public Policy.* Boulder: Westview Press, 137–48.

Ladson-Billings, Gloria. 1994. *The Dreamkeepers: Successful Teachers of African American Children.* San Francisco: Jossey-Bass.

Lawrence, D. H. 1915. *The Rainbow.* New York: The Modern Library.

Lawrence-Lightfoot, Sara. 1994. *I've Known Rivers: Lives of Loss and Liberation.* Reading, Mass.: Addison-Wesley.

Lorde, Audre. 1984. *Sister Outsider.* Trumansburg, N.Y.: The Crossing Press.

Lortie, Dan C. 1975. *Schoolteacher: A Sociological Study.* Chicago: University of Chicago Press.

Maher, Frances A., and Mary Kay Tetreault. 1994. *The Feminist Classroom: An Inside Look at How Professors and Students Are Transforming Higher Education for a Diverse Society.* New York: Basic Books.

———. 1997. Learning in the Dark: How Assumptions of Whiteness Shape Classroom Knowledge. *Harvard Educational Review* 67, 2: 321–49.

Martin, Jane Roland. 1992. *Schoolhome: Rethinking Schools for Changing Families.* Cambridge, Mass.: Harvard University Press.

Matchan, Linda. 25 January 2000. "Real Boys Should Cry." *The Boston Globe.* E1, E6.

McIntosh, Peggy. 1989. White Privilege: Unpacking the Invisible Knapsack. *Peace and Freedom* July/August: 10–12.

Middleton, Sue. 1993. *Educating Feminists: Life Histories and Pedagogy.* New York: Teachers College Press.

Morrison, Toni. 1992. *Playing in the Dark: Whiteness and the Literary Imagination.* Cambridge, Mass.: Harvard University Press.

Neill, A. S. 1960. *Summerhill.* New York: Hart.

Noddings, Nel. 1992. *The Challenge to Care in Schools: An Alternative Approach to Education.* New York: Teachers College Press.

Paley, Vivian. 1989. *White Teacher.* Cambridge, Mass.: Harvard University Press.

Postman, Neil, and Charles Weingartner. 1969. *Teaching as a Subversive Activity.* New York: Dell.

Reinharz, Shulamit. 1992. *Feminist Methods in Social Research.* New York: Oxford University Press.

Rich, Adrienne. 1979. *On Lies, Secrets, and Silences: Selected Prose, 1966–1978.* New York: Norton.

———. 1986. Compulsory Heterosexuality and Lesbian Existence. In Adrienne Rich, *Blood, Bread, and Poetry, Selected Prose, 1979–1985.* New York: Norton.

Riley, Denise. 1990. *"Am I That Name?": Feminism and the Category of 'Women' in History.* Minneapolis: The University of Minnesota Press.

Sadker, Myra, and David Sadker. 1994. *Failing at Fairness: How Our Schools Cheat Girls.* New York: Simon & Schuster.

Seuss, Dr. 1990. *Oh, the Places You'll Go!* New York: Random House.

Sklar, Kathryn Kish. 1973. *Catherine Beecher: A Study in American Domesticity.* New York: Norton.

Spender, Dale. 1982. *Invisible Woman: The Schooling Scandal.* London: Writers and Readers Publishing Cooperative Society.

Spock, Dr. Benjamin, and Michael B. Rothenburg. 1946, 1985. *Baby and Child Care.* New York: E. P. Dutton.

Thorne, Barrie. 1993. *Gender Play: Girls and Boys in School.* New Brunswick, N.J.: Rutgers University Press.

Titone, Connie, and Karen Maloney. 1999. *Women's Philosophies of Education: Thinking Through Our Mothers.* Upper Saddle River, N.J.: Prentice-Hall.

Tong, Rosemary. 1989. *Feminist Thought: A Comprehensive Introduction.* Boulder: Westview Press.

Weiler, Kathleen. 1988. *Women Teaching for Change: Gender, Class, and Power.* New York: Bergin and Garvey.

———. 1989. Women's History and the History of Women Teachers. *Journal of Education* 171, 3: 9–30.

———. (1991). Freire and a Feminist Pedagogy of Difference. *Harvard Educational Review* 61, 4: 449–74.

Woolf, Virginia. 1938, 1966. *Three Guineas.* New York: Harcourt Brace.

Index

About the Author

Carla Washburne Rensenbrink, a classroom teacher for eighteen years, has taught classes in education and feminist teaching at Harvard Graduate School of Education and at the University of New Hampshire.